Praise for Unbinding Christianity

If you have found it impossible to continue believing in some of the doctrines the church has taught to be essential and don't know if you can continue being a Christian, Jan Linn offers some much needed guidance. He invites readers to think along with him as he makes distinctions between believing in doctrines and having value-enlivened belief, between being a Christian and being Christian. His message is that just because your integrity demands you give up on some traditional Christian ideas doesn't mean you need to become a Christian dropout.

—The Rev. Craig Watts, D.Min, author of *Bowing Toward Babylon*

Unbinding Christianity is a thought-provoking argument for expansion of Christianity's often employed litmus tests of inclusion and rejection. Jan Linn addresses this complex issue in a clear, concise, and easily accessible manner. A great read!

—Joshua Santana, Attorney-at-Law

This book is a wake-up call to all of us who choose to follow Jesus, a challenge for us to rethink what it truly means to be Christian. Jan Linn's thesis is simple, yet profound—it is what we do on a daily basis, not what we believe, that is the core of a Christian life.

—Heather Cargill, Psy.D., Licensed Clinical Psychologist

In a biblically well-informed and a life-experience challenging way, *Unbinding Christianity* explores a central question: Are we called to follow the values of the life Jesus lived or are we merely following a set of beliefs the Church has offered? This book offers hope to those who have felt excluded by the latter and want help with following the culturally-challenging way that Jesus lived.

—Kevin Campbell, Director, US Long Term Disaster Recovery, Habitat For Humanity

Being Christian, it seems to me, is less a set of beliefs and more a way of life. While I have believed that for many years, Jan Linn's clear, concise, and compelling book clarifies why this is so, and how the very future of the faith depends on its recognition. This book will benefit everyone concerned about the future of Christianity and the future of the church.

—The Rev. Nathan Wilson, Director of Communications, Christian Theological Seminary

Jan Linn argues that the Christian faith has become distorted by a focus on beliefs rather than the values Jesus taught. For many Christians his message will be welcomed with relief, even joy, as they struggle between their resistance to certain required Christian beliefs and their love for their church.

—Judy Foster, Ph.D., Professor of English, St. Cloud State University, Retired

Jan Linn offers a much-needed challenge to those who claim to follow Jesus: move beyond easy "believe-ism" to embrace the demands the gospel places on us. Linn argues Jesus asks us to live like him, not merely to believe like him. This is a crucial insight at this pivotal moment in our history.

—The Rev. Derek Penwell, Ph.D., author of *Outlandish: An Unlikely Messiah, A Messy Ministry, and the Call to Mobilize*

Unbinding
Christianity

Unbinding Christianity

Choosing the Values of Jesus over the Beliefs of the Church

Jan G. Linn

Universal Publishers
Irvine • Boca Raton

*Unbinding Christianity: Choosing the Values of Jesus
over the Beliefs of the Church*

Universal Publishers, Inc.
Irvine • Boca Raton
USA • 2020
www.Universal-Publishers.com

ISBN: 978-1-62734-292-6 (pbk.)
ISBN: 978-1-62734-293-3 (ebk.)

Typeset by Medlar Publishing Solutions Pvt Ltd, India
Cover design by Paul Champie

Publisher's Cataloging-in-Publication Data
available at the United States Library of Congress

For

The Gathering House

Contents

Acknowledgments

Thanking my wife, Joy, for her role in everything I write usually comes last. I finally realized that was backwards. She should be the first person I acknowledge. Ultimately she is the reason my work sees the light of day. She has a keen eye for mistakes in the text and a marvelous sense of what does and does not read well. For this particular book, though, her years of experience in ministry and her understanding of what being Christian means have contributed far beyond style and tone. Her substantive contributions run through every chapter. More than anything, though, she has always helped me to believe in my own writing and never to question its value. That is what loving support truly means.

The Reverend David Digby was the first person I asked to read this material. It was in its early stage, but I knew of no one whose objective theological assessment of my argument I trusted more than his. Not only did he encourage me to keep writing, but offered insights that provided needed direction when I seemed to be floundering. For that kind of help, and the fact that we have been friends and colleagues in ministry for many years is something I hope never to take for granted.

And then there is Bill Blackwell. It is rare for a writer to have a best friend who has a copy editor's eye without ever having worked as one professionally, though he does hold an advanced degree in literature. In addition, he has the strength of intellect to speak candidly about the quality of my argument and the efficacy of the writing. Perhaps most important, though, is that Bill lives a life that is consistent with Christian principles and values without having been raised in a church or attended one as an adult on any regular basis. He is, in fact, precisely the kind of person to whom I am hoping this book will appeal.

I also want to thank my publisher, Jeff Young, for being willing to take on this project. We had worked together on *What's Wrong With The Christian Right*, a very satisfying experience for me from beginning to end. Because I had some unconventional ideas regarding this book's publication, Jeff was the first person I wanted to contact to see if he would at least give me a hearing about them. Obviously, he did more than that, and once again the collaboration has been a pleasure throughout.

Endorsements

There is nothing unusual about endorsements for a book, except in the case of this book there is. Endorsements function to assure potential readers that a book has been judged by qualified critics to have credibility on the subject and is worth the time to read. The credibility of endorsements depends, of course, on the people giving them, usually scholars and/or people who possess expertise in the subject matter of the book. The value of an endorsement is obviously enhanced significantly if it is written by someone with name recognition.

During more than thirty-five years of writing, I have been fortunate to have secured a wide spectrum of endorsements from people I respect and admire and in a few instances people well known to the public. For this book, though, I chose to approach soliciting endorsements in a different way, by asking people who represent the book's intended reading audience to evaluate it, and, if willing, to add their endorsement. Specifically, I wanted to ask past and present congregational ministers who bear primary responsibility for teaching church members what being Christian means to consider an endorsement. More specifically, I sought those who exemplify the pastor/scholar model in their practice of ministry. There was a time when pastor/scholar was the model to which young ministers aspired. Today only a few do, or stay with it if they try, because of the demands of modern congregational life that amount to expecting ministers to be all things to all people. The clergy who gave endorsements are beloved pastors and respected thinkers. Each of them is an advocate for social, economic, and racial justice. At the same time they have authored books and academic articles, and in one instance writes a regular column for a major mid-western city newspaper. These are ministers who are well qualified to assess the book's distinction between being **a** Christian and being Christian because they embody it in their own lives.

The non-clergy endorsements share equal status with the ones written by the pastor/scholars. One of them lives and moves and has his being in the ministry called Habitat for Humanity. He didn't study for the ministry, but he did choose to make service to others his life's vocation. Daily he works with and on behalf of families that need a safe and respectable place to live. He may or may not attend church regularly, but his life teaches and preaches the core message of this book, that being Christian should be defined by the values Jesus lived and taught.

Another one is a highly successful attorney in Kentucky who is a first-generation American of Puerto Rican heritage, is active in a mainline denominational church, and whose law practice includes providing pro bono counsel and legal representation to workers and migrants who would otherwise be at the mercy of a legal system that can be unmerciful and unfair. He knows the difference between being **a** Christian and being Christian, a distinction the book will explain in detail.

The third one is a highly respected child psychologist who came to organized religion as an adult, allowing her to experience first hand the struggle to be Christian while not being able to embrace various claims the church told her she should believe. In addition, throughout her practice she continues to confront some of the obstacles parental religious beliefs can create in her efforts to help children recover from infant and early childhood emotional and physical trauma.

The final non-clergy endorser was until recently Professor of English at a state university, and a writer herself. She is from a small southern city and raised in traditional Christianity. It became obvious to her as a young adult that she did not believe what she had been taught were the basic tenets of Christian belief. During this same time she was developing a growing commitment to social justice while not seeing much evidence that her church shared that commitment. Eventually she abandoned traditional Christianity for Unitarian Universalism where thinking was valued rather than resisted and theological fringes were seen as normal. Since that time she has become a major leader in her congregation and a visible advocate for social justice in her community. She said from the beginning that she would read the book as a Unitarian Universalist which would shape and inform any endorsement she might write. That sealed the deal for me.

And then there was the endorsement that got away. This rather intriguing story is too long to tell, but the gist of it is that a Christian scholar was unexpectedly given a copy of the manuscript. Much to my surprise he read it and then took the time to write to me with his suggestions for revision. He appreciated the argument I was making, he said, but had some major concerns with my thesis. I took his critique seriously, making some of the revisions he suggested and then sent them to him for further review. He seemed pleased with my effort, but was candid in saying that he still had some reservations about the core argument I was making. He then added, "But to reiterate. You're saying something important that lots of people will experience as—if I may say so—salvific."

We exchanged more emails, and when the manuscript was completed I took the bold step and asked if he would consider writing an endorsement. He declined, or, in his word, "demurred." because he was still concerned about the sharp distinction he thought the book made between doctrine and practice. Were he to write an endorsement, he explained, he would need to address his concerns which, he believed, would defeat the purpose of the endorsement.

I share this story because it is a testimony to the personal integrity of this fine scholar and man. It also underscores the reason endorsements matter and can aid potential readers in evaluating a book. They are not taken lightly by the people who write them, which is why they do serve the interests of potential readers in evaluating a book. Ironically, his refusal also points to the reason I wrote the book in the first place, to challenge the church's beliefs-based Christianity that often limits this kind of honest and open exchange. A preoccupation with church authority has stood in the way of intellectual debate and exploration, something I think has played a significant role in the church's decline today. Perhaps this book will nudge all of us who claim the name Christian to a place where beliefs are respected even as values define what it means to be Christian.

Why A Book Like This

I have written this book for anyone who is Christian, has been Christian, or for any number of reasons has an interest in Christianity. But it is written most especially for Christians who don't believe everything the church has told them they should believe to be a Christian. My thesis is simple: You can be as Christian as anyone else without letting the church tell you what beliefs you must hold to qualify. I describe it as the difference between being Christian that is focused on living by the values Jesus lived and taught and being **a** Christian that is defined by "right" beliefs. This difference is about an understanding of Christianity that doesn't dismiss Christian beliefs, but is free of the church wrapping Christianity into a small package of creeds, doctrines, dogma, and right beliefs that has squeezed the life out of it for many people who cannot accept those beliefs as "gospel."

The challenge as I see it is what I call the unbinding of Christianity that shifts its meaning from beliefs, creeds, and doctrines to the values Jesus actually talked about. There is a story in the gospel of John about a man named Lazarus who suddenly becomes ill and dies whose ending speaks directly to what I think Christianity desperately needs. Lazarus and his two sisters, Mary and Martha, lived in a small town called Bethany a couple of miles from Jerusalem. When their brother dies, Mary and Martha send word to Jesus of what has happened. Staying in the region around the Jordan River where he had been teaching, for some unknown reason Jesus delays going to Bethany four days. By the time he arrives Lazarus had already been wrapped in grave clothes and placed in a tomb similar to the one in which Jesus himself would be placed after his crucifixion. Eventually Jesus goes with Mary and Martha to the tomb where, the story says, Jesus broke down and wept. He then instructs some men to roll the stone from the grave's entrance, after which he surprises the crowd by calling Lazarus to come out. To everyone's astonishment Lazarus appears at the tomb's entrance. Jesus immediately says to those gathered, "Unbind him, and let him go" (John 11:1-44).

How ironic that all these centuries later the simple message of Jesus about how to be in the world without being of it needs to be set free of the wrappings of death much as Lazarus was. Not that the church's statements of faith were intended to function as grave clothing, but I think that is precisely what has happened. As a result, today's Christianity is for all practical purposes a religion about Jesus while his own words about the values by which Christians can and should live have been pushed aside. What is more, the divisions that separate American Christians from one another today are largely rooted in the fault lines of beliefs about Jesus, God, the Holy Spirit, the future of the world, and the like. It often seems as if the church is determined to argue and fight over beliefs about Jesus rather than focusing on equipping people to live their lives the way he lived his.

Adding to the problem is that over the centuries church hierarchy has become less tolerant of dissent and more determined to exercise its authority and power to force conformity of belief. If you grew up in the church you were probably taught traditional Christian beliefs such as Jesus was born of the Virgin Mary, was God in the flesh, died for the sins of the world, was raised from the dead, and will one day return to judge the living and the dead. It is possible your church allowed you to question these beliefs, but it is more likely that you were told to accept them at face value. You may still be in a church that is saying this, or you may have dropped out for that very reason. What I hope this book will show you is that there is an alternative to this kind of Christianity that focuses on values instead of beliefs. Before we get there, though, let's put our discussion in some historical context.

In significant ways the Protestant Reformation of the 16th century was a successful challenge to a beliefs-based faith, but the diversity of beliefs it produced happened more unintentionally than intentionally, a by-product of freedom from church authority that had forced conformity of beliefs for

centuries. While the door to theological diversity in today's Catholic par-
ishes is opened slightly, theological debate and disagreement is more preva-
lent within and among Protestant denominations and independent groups.
This in fact is a major reason for Protestant splintering in the first place.
It is why Christian beliefs themselves represent stunning diversity across and
within denominational lines.

The upside is that modern Protestant Christians are exercising their
right to think for themselves when it comes to matters of faith and morals
rather than allowing a church or denomination to tell them what to believe.
Instead of seeing this as something positive, though, many church leaders
see this as a bad thing. If they happen to be in positions of authority, they
often become quite defensive of the church's right to define Christian beliefs
everyone should embrace. I think this has been a major factor in the massive
exodus from the church we have witnessed in the last forty plus years, and
now we are seeing its effects on the credibility of Christianity itself.

I am not suggesting that there are no normative beliefs in Christianity,
only that the history and diversity of their development don't justify using
them as tests of faith or fellowship. They can serve as statements of faith,
which interestingly enough was the original purpose of church creeds in the
first place.[1] Conformity of beliefs has never served Christianity well, mainly
because it divides rather than unites Christians. It doesn't have to be this
way. The Christian faith is quite capable of being examined and challenged
and re-evaluated, if it understands itself to be about values instead of beliefs.

I am not talking about a new Christianity. I am talking about the focus
Christianity should have had in the first place. Religions promote specific
beliefs, but my argument is that the words of Jesus make it abundantly clear
that following him is about a particular way of living in the world. Not that
the church doesn't know this. It just chose to emphasize right beliefs, in large
part because right beliefs served the goal of establishing ecclesial authority
that in turn helped maintain at least some control over what Christians
believed.

---

[1] In his argument for the value of creeds in the book, *The Creed: What Christians Believe
and Why it Matters* (Image Books Reprint, 2004), Luke Timothy Johnson makes the point
that the value and role of creeds has suffered from the way the church has used them as tests
of faith.

One of the criticisms I have already encountered in conversations about my thesis is that I am making an argument that is a distinction without a difference. "We live the way we believe," I have been told, making what we believe essential to living the lifestyle to which Jesus calls Christians to live. But that misses the point. I am not saying that beliefs don't matter or have no influence on what people do. My contention is that beliefs don't matter as much as the church says and not in the way the church insists they do. A values-based Christianity is not in conflict with beliefs. If anything, a focus on values creates an environment that gives beliefs room to breathe and flourish. A focus on beliefs has the opposite effect on values, constricting their power to the point of nearly choking the life out of them.

The roots of my realization that beliefs and values represent a distinction that reflects a huge difference in people's lives go back to growing up in a racist Southern culture where churches taught a form of Christianity that did not believe segregation was inconsistent with being Christian, but that is getting ahead of myself. As we begin I simply want to highlight the primary focus traditional Christian teaching places in beliefs when Christians would be better served by a focus on values.

If you self-identify as Christian or once did because you were raised as one, you have encountered first-hand this emphasis on right beliefs I find so troubling. In the course of my ministry I think I have met about every kind of Christian there is. I know Christians who believe what they believe and nothing is ever going to change them. I know other Christians who are the opposite of the ones just described. They are not sure what they believe so what they believe is pliable and flexible. Still others have strong beliefs, but are constantly reading and studying to learn more than they know and have no timidity in adjusting what they believe to new information. What all these people have in common is that beliefs matter to them. What differentiates them is that members of the first group have a faith defined by beliefs while the others at minimum are uncomfortable with the beliefs they have been told Christians should believe.

The nature of religion is such that diversity is always present whether it is embraced, resisted, or ignored. This book seeks to make a case for diversity in beliefs being core to the kind of Christianity that is focused on following Jesus rather than "believing in" him or explaining who he was. By the time you finish reading I hope you will at the very least understand that the message of Jesus can be set free from all the wrappings of beliefs that have squeezed the life out of it for people who refuse to have "blind faith." There is a Christian path forward that makes freedom of thought a gift of faith rather than something to be feared. Christianity focused on living rather than believing need never be afraid of people whose faith is open minded and open ended.

At the same time, though, I want to say unequivocally that I am not at all interested in trying to persuade anyone to give up something they fervently believe or believe in. Changing beliefs is an inside job that happens when people are ready for it and usually not a moment before. It can happen for a variety of reasons, but it seldom happens by someone trying to persuade another person to change his or her mind. More important is the fact that trying to persuade you or anyone to abandon one belief in favor of another misses the point of the book entirely. I don't offer alternatives to replace the "right" beliefs you may have been taught or have heard define Christianity. Instead, I try to explain why a beliefs-based faith takes you down the wrong road and, thus, hinders rather than helps you live as a Christian in the modern world.

There are, then, three basic claims I make in the book. The first is the need to understand and accept the nature of beliefs. The second is the need to realize that the church defining what it means to be a Christian by beliefs was a mistake with enormous, even tragic, consequences. The third is the need to see that Jesus said very little about beliefs, but said a lot about living a particular kind of lifestyle based on values he lived and taught to others. What I hope you will discover if you are among those who have trouble believing what the church says you must believe is that you are not the problem. The church is. As you will see, I have a few things to say about the church throughout the book because it is impossible to talk about Christianity without mentioning the church. At the same time, the real focus is telling you about being Christian in spite of what you believe or don't believe, not because of it. In these pages I suggest an alternative to a Christian faith bound and weighted down by creeds, doctrines, and dogmas—formal and informal.

It will help you to bear in mind as you go that the chapters are interconnected, succeeding ones building upon the ones that come before them and questions arising in one chapter being answered in a different one. By the time you reach the end, though, I think you will have a clear sense of where you are and how you got there. My goal is not that you agree with what I have written, only that it helps you to think for yourself about matters of beliefs while understanding that being Christian has less to do with what you believe at any point in your life and more to do with how you live your life all the time. In the process I hope you will see what I see, that Christianity is a rich faith tradition that doesn't have all the answers, but does raise many of the right questions, and further, that its basic message is not about "right beliefs," but about "right living."

1

Unintended Consequences

L et's begin with the obvious, that Jesus was not a Christian, he was a Jew. This means he was raised to believe that faithfulness to God revealed itself in the way you treat others, whether they be your family, neighbors, strangers, or even your enemies. It is no accident, then, that as an itinerate rabbi this is how Jesus lived and what he taught that served to challenge a Judaism that by the first century had become Temple based and focused on rituals and the observance of Holy Days. It is ironic that Christianity has followed a similar path to Judaism by defining itself by beliefs, "right" beliefs, as it turned out, while neglecting what Jesus called "the weightier matters of the law" that have to do with behavior.

That Christianity is defined by beliefs is an enigma when you consider the nature of beliefs themselves. A belief is a belief, not a fact. Once a belief becomes a fact, it is no longer a belief. Thus, everything anyone—including me—believes about Jesus (or anything related to religion) is a belief, which means it may be true, then again, it may be false. Unfortunately, many churches, and thus, many more Christians, have chosen to ignore the fundamental nature of beliefs. In the process they are missing the power of believing I will talk about in the next chapter because they are too concerned about "proving" that what they believe is true. That, of course, is precisely what you cannot do with beliefs because by nature they do not yield themselves to proof.

A consequence of not understanding or appreciating the nature of beliefs is the temptation to make judgments about who is or is not a Christian.

I have been down this road more than once, where I have been told that I am not a "real" Christian because of things I believe or don't believe. It's true, of course, that I believe and don't believe many things I was taught to believe growing up in the church. I once believed Jesus was born of a virgin, for example. Not anymore. I believed he was God. Not anymore. I believed he died for my sins. Not anymore. I believed he was coming back like a thief in the night, taking some back to heaven, leaving more behind. Not anymore. I believed Jesus was the only means of salvation. Not anymore. I believed the Bible was the word of God, infallible and inerrant in the original. Not anymore.

These changes in my beliefs have not made me less Christian, they have in fact strengthened my resolve to stand firmly in the Christian tradition. What has changed is that I now attend much more to being Christian rather than being **a** Christian, a distinction I will explain in more detail later. Here I need only say that the former focuses on values and the latter on beliefs. Making that distinction has been one of the most freeing discoveries I have ever experienced, one that was hiding in plain sight that for too long I failed to see. I hope this book will help you see it much sooner in your life than I did in mine.

The focus on right beliefs has had more than a few tragic consequences since the beginning of the Christian movement. Arius, Bishop of Alexandria, was declared a heretic for teaching that Jesus was not equal or "of the same substance" as God. A theologian named Pelagius suffered the same fate when he argued that "original sin" (as articulated by St. Augustine, Bishop of Hippo) did not prevent human beings from choosing between good and evil, a moral decision he believed they were quite capable of making. Such controversies and the rise of the authority of the bishop of Rome led to a permanent split between Western Christianity and Eastern Orthodoxy. Add corruption to the conflict over power and authority and you get the Protestant Reformation, which itself immediately began splintering into thousands of sects, congregations, and eventually denominations because of controversies over beliefs.

A preoccupation with right beliefs led John Calvin, the most dominant of all Reformation theologians, to give his blessing to his Calvinist followers burning Michael Servetus at the stake in the 16th century because they considered him a heretic for disagreeing with what they believed. It is also why anti-Semitism swept over Western Europe and laid the foundation for the Holocaust and the church's complicity in it, and why New England Puritan preachers supported the utter destruction of native American culture. It is what happens when you have a religion about Jesus instead of a community of faith living the teachings of Jesus.

The Believers Mistake

Symptomatic of both the success of a beliefs-based Christianity and the negative consequences it has caused is the fact that it is common today to hear Christians referred to as "believers." There is so much that is wrong with that adjective that it is difficult to know where to start, but perhaps the most important one is the fact that there is no reason to think Jesus called people to be believers. He, instead, called them to follow him as people committed to doing the will of God in their lives as faithfully as possible. That was his primary concern. Yet the Christianity most of us know is a message about beliefs. If you have thought of yourself as a "believer," you may still be determined to do the will of God as a way of showing you are Christian, but that is not the way the church has normally defined being Christian.

I find this emphasis on right beliefs in Christianity an enigma, not least because beliefs regularly prove themselves to be shifting sand that makes rigidity of beliefs the alternative for those unwilling to accept the subjective nature of beliefs. Beliefs have not only been shown to be wrong, they are often false and/or dangerous. The church itself has even admitted that things it once believed were actually false and things it said were false turned out to be true. Its 1642 condemnation of Galileo is a perfect example. Convinced the sun rotated around the earth, the church condemned Copernicus and Galileo for saying the opposite was true. Pope John Paul II declared the controversy over in 1992 by officially declaring the church was in error. It would have been better had Pope John Paul admitted that the church's preoccupation with right beliefs is what led to the mistake it made regarding Copernicus and Galileo.

I know the world of beliefs-based faith because I was raised in it. As was probably true with most of the kids I grew up with, I never thought much about what my home church taught me until I made the decision to become a minister and entered seminary. In short order I encountered the world of diverse beliefs, but strangely I was not bothered by that in the least as many students with similar backgrounds were. At the same time, I had to confront the fact that most of the "right beliefs" about which I was quite certain were not shared by my classmates who I knew were just as Christian as I was. Instead of being upset with my professors about what they were teaching, I was upset by what my home church had taught me that no longer made any sense. Why were they afraid of other points of view, and the pursuit of truth itself?

That was only half the battle I had. I also admitted to myself that the people I loved and who loved me, especially my pastor and his wife, were racists. Like virtually every other southern white congregation, my home church not only supported segregation, it practiced it. Lay leaders went so far as to position themselves at the entrance of the sanctuary at all worship services in order to prevent any black individual, family or group from entering. They sincerely and wrongly believed that racial integration would lead to intermarriage that would result in the creation of a mongrel race.

That was a traumatic time for me—and all Christians—as the disconnect between being a Christian and being a decent human being was like a neon sign flashing on and off. It was stunning that so many southern Christians embraced the racist belief in white supremacy and its inevitable by-product, racial segregation. Much of what I believe today about the inadequacy of a beliefs-based faith stems from those years of watching so many Christians betray everything they said they believed and believed in because of a beliefs-based faith. They were not bad people. They were people who sincerely believed what the church told them to believe that never connected being a Christian with racial justice. You cannot grow up in such a culture without wearing the scars of truth cutting away the skin of institutional Christianity that could not do justice, love kindness, or walk humbly before God (Micah 6:8) because of what the church taught its members to believe.

At the same time, there were other white Christians who supported racial justice and stood with black Americans in the fight to make liberty and justice for all a genuine reality. These white Christians were able to break through and free of the restraints of a beliefs-based faith to see that at the end of the day what truly mattered to them as Christians was whether they did what was right. Whatever beliefs they had were secondary to that.

I am thinking of the wife of a district court judge in a small Virginia town who when I moved there was the first person named by others as someone committed to social justice, especially racial equality, while being in a congregation that was silent, if not complicit, in racial and social injustice in the town.

The kind of raw racism I witnessed as a young pastor was and still is described as an example of hypocrisy, but I think the problem goes much deeper than that. A beliefs-based Christianity inevitably bifurcates beliefs and behavior because holding on to right beliefs is a standard easier to measure, and far easier to teach. I confessed Jesus as my savior and Lord without thinking about what that required of me in actual behavior. I was, of course, a child at the time, but it would have been no different had I been adult. Open racists made "the good confession" in my home church and didn't miss a beat. When I was twelve I worked as a "go-fer" for an elder in my church who was a professional carpenter. He and I were both boxing fans. The morning after Floyd Patterson knocked out Ingemar Johansson to regain the heavy weight championship, I asked him what he thought of the results. He responded with a racist rant peppered with profanity that stunned me into silence. The next Sunday he was teaching Sunday School as he usually did and praying at the Communion table as if he had never said what he did a few days before, or that it mattered that he had.

Writing all of this seems a bit surreal today, but it was very real fifty years ago and underscores the fundamental point that a beliefs-based faith is a source of trouble and division, conflict and judgmentalism, all of which is avoidable only when a shift in thinking occurs that focuses on values. Beliefs-based Christianity ignores the very definition of the word "belief"— the conviction of the truth of a statement or opinion—by speaking as if the degree of a conviction influences the truth of a claim. But common sense is all you need to understand that being convinced that something is true does not make it true. This is especially important when it comes to religious beliefs because religion evokes passion which can result in blurring the line between conviction and truth. A common fault among people of faith is forgetting the obvious—that beliefs are always and only beliefs, not facts; opinions are opinions, not facts. Religious beliefs, like all beliefs, are true only in the sense that they fall outside the realm of provability. If a belief is proven to be true or false, it is no longer a belief.

The gospel writers tell the story of the disciples as well as Jesus and in doing so they leave no doubt that their faith in Jesus was based on values, not beliefs. These fisherman, tax collectors, prostitutes, wives, and mothers who responded to his call to follow him did so without knowing what to believe about him. Nor did they show they had learned much after three years when he met them again after the resurrection (Acts 1:6). It didn't matter. They believed in what he said and felt the presence of God when they were with him. That was enough to lead them to commit themselves to his way of life at all costs. They could follow him even though they didn't know for sure if he was the messiah for whom they had waiting. He had not done anything they expected the messiah to do, yet they followed him before his crucifixion and after his resurrection anyway.

Beliefs change, evolve, mature because they are dynamic. They can be conservative or liberal, Catholic, Protestant, or Orthodox, Jewish, Muslim, Hindu, Buddhist, anything and always out of reach of proof. The consequence of this reality is that all beliefs have the potential of being right and being wrong, yet either way they can and usually do impact your attitudes and actions. In other words, beliefs have consequences, but those consequences do not make a belief anything more than a belief. Believing doesn't make anything true other than the fact that you believe it is. In other words, anything you believe carries the possibility of not being true, and that means when you believe something you are taking the risk that you are wrong. That is precisely why no belief should be set in concrete so as to be untouchable in being questioned or challenged. Every belief should be under scrutiny because everything we humans believe always and forever carries the possibility of being off the mark.

One of the reasons Christians are defensive about things they believe is that they have an emotional attachment to what they believe that is often stronger than they realize. That in turn can blind them to the temptation to equate beliefs with facts. At the end of the day what you believe means you have chosen one thing rather than another. There is nothing divine about that choice. It's yours, but it may not be someone else's. Remember that and you will do no harm. Forget it and you may do immense harm. This is the way faith works because faith is always a choice. If you are a person of faith, it is because you have chosen to be, not because the evidence led you to that conclusion. You may interpret evidence to support what you believe, but interpretations are not facts, nor is faith limited to evidence that leans one way or the other. Religious faith presumes something is true until it is proven not to be. In some instances no such evidence of proof is even possible.

Freedom of Thought

One of the casualties of the church's beliefs-based faith is the fear of and resistance to freedom of thought. The counsel most traditional churches give you is (to quote an old hymn) "trust and obey, for there's no other way, to be happy in Jesus, but to trust and obey." That kind of sentiment expressed so often in gospel songs is both bad counsel and bad theology. The way you make faith your own is to think for yourself, standing over against a Christianity that centuries ago morphed into a religion that demanded conformity of belief in large measure to establish its own authority and power. What you and all thoughtful people know is that the pursuit of truth is not only consistent with faith, but essential to its integrity and credibility. What is more, focusing on values defuses any conflict between faith and truth by doing just the opposite. Values free you to be free in the pursuit of truth because your trust in God and in the teachings of Jesus is not put in jeopardy by yet uncovered truth. Faith represents your willingness to believe in God without knowing with certainty that God exists because the values that define your faith are worth living no matter where the pursuit of truth leads.

The danger inherent in the failure to understand that the church has made Christianity about beliefs when Jesus talked about values is the ease with which you can confuse the validity of beliefs with the impact the power of believing can have on you. In the next chapter I want to focus on the power of believing, ironically as a way to show that it has nothing to do with whether or not what you believe is true, false, good, or bad.

2

The Power of Believing

I was nine years old when I became a Christian for the first time. Back then it was called joining the church. In my tradition you went forward at the end of a worship service, usually Sunday morning, and made what my pastor called the "good confession of faith." You were then baptized by immersion to seal the deal. I became Christian when I realized that what I believed was secondary to how I lived my life. The difference between the two could not have been more stark. As a child I trusted that the traditional beliefs I was being taught were true and shouldn't be questioned because they were what the Bible said. The warning was that once I began questioning one thing, I would question everything. Scared into fearing going to hell, I remember trying very hard to follow that advice. The irony was that my home church was more right than the members ever realized. Once I did begin to question what I had been taught I never stopped, a process I discovered was key to putting away my childhood faith in exchange for one that did not crumble in the face of hard questions.

The truth I discovered about the faith I had when I first became a Christian was that it was rooted in the church's message that was and still is like a house of cards. Take away one thing and the whole thing falls down. If Jesus was not born of a virgin, for example, that means Joseph was his biological father and Jesus was just a man as I am. How, then, could he have been divine, of the same "substance" of God, as the creeds say? No wonder I was told not to question anything. It did lead to a healthy skepticism about beliefs that didn't make sense to me. Essentially, the first time I became a

Christian it was based on the things I was taught to believe about Jesus. When I became Christian it was based on what Jesus himself actually said and did. That the two were not only different, but in significant ways contradictory, was the key realization for me of just how far off the track church teaching was.

In my years in ministry as a preacher and a teacher I have met many Christians like me for whom what the church teaches is difficult to accept. More than a few wonder if they can say they are still Christian given what they believe and don't believe now. Others are no longer sure they even want to be considered a Christian. When seventy-five percent of Christians no longer attend church on a regular basis, and more than a third of the population under the age of forty identify as religiously "unaffiliated" (at one point in our history nearly eighty-five percent of all Americans self-identified as Christian), the church has a problem with what it is saying—and doing.[2]

I wrote this book for the people just mentioned above because I would have benefited from having a book like this one during a time when I could not stop asking questions about God, Jesus, the Bible, and the like. I would not have felt as isolated as I did had someone more theologically informed and with more experience in ministry assured me that the church didn't have all the answers. It didn't occur to me then that the church's understanding of Christianity might be off the mark, in fact, way off the mark. The choice I thought I had was to believe or not believe what the church said about what I should believe, and if I chose the latter I was not a real Christian.

That is not a choice anyone who wants to be a Christian should have to make. But the church is forcing it on people, making them choose between letting the church tell them what to believe or thinking for themselves. That most of them have walked away has been their response to that forced choice. In truth, the church has often been afraid of open minds that ask tough questions since it penned the first creed (Nicene) in the early fourth century. For centuries the general population did not question what the church said. Then the Protestant Reformation exploded in 1517 and all hell broke

---

[2] The most reliable source for church attendance is denominational records that have measured regular attendance between 25 to 30 percent for several years. The last year the percentage was this high is 1990. (https://web.archive.org/web/20110709082644/http://www.gc.cuny.edu/faculty/research_briefs/aris/key_findings.hm)

loose among the peasants. Europe was never the same. Church authority remained formidable in Western Europe for two more centuries until the Age of Enlightenment vaulted the arts, literature, science, and learning in general to the forefront of life. At every turn questioning church authority was met with persecution in order to maintain control of the populace. New England Puritanism was heir to this kind of Christianity, only to be eventually undermined by freedoms guaranteed by the Constitution and western expansion that allowed people to move away from church control, and even influence.

I know the church's internal struggles over authority and external rejection of its teachings well because I have spent my entire adulthood in its service. I also know that its problems are largely of its own making, starting with the mistake of insisting on conformity of belief by anyone who wanted to become a Christian. In the process it focused less and less on the what Jesus taught, specifically the values that reflected the will of God on earth. The core argument of this book is that values instead of right beliefs are what identify what it means to be Christian. If you are among the majority of Christians who for whatever reason have dropped out of the church, have never gone, or still attend but often wonder why you do, what you will find here is a different way of understanding what it means to be a Christian that will take the focus away from beliefs and put it on the kind of life you are to live as a Christian. That doesn't make being Christian easier, but you will see that it makes more sense than what the church has told you and in the process will free you of theological baggage you don't need to be dragging around.

To get there, however, I need to start at a place that may strike you as a bit odd, with the role the power of believing can and often does play in people's lives. The impact believing something has on all of us is actually quite incredible and is something worthy of respect, if not admiration. At the same time, people often confuse how believing affects their lives with the validity of what they believe. That is a serious mistake because it contradicts the nature of beliefs, their value and their limitations, something I will discuss in detail in the next chapter. Exploring the impact the power of believing has on people is necessary before we get into that.

A final note. Exceedingly helpful in my understanding that Christianity defined by beliefs is off the mark has been the work of the brilliant American scholar, Joseph Campbell. Campbell was one of the world's foremost scholars on comparative mythology and comparative religion, serving as Professor of Literature at Sarah Lawrence college for more than thirty years. He first gained widespread notoriety through a series of PBS interviews with journalist Bill Moyers in the 1980s.[3] Campbell's work revolved around the subject he spent his life studying, the power of myth. His insights opened my eyes to why a beliefs-based Christianity is unable to serve the spiritual needs of people today. Upon first exposure to Campbell's thinking, some people find it too esoteric to have practical value or, worse, is a threat to religion in general and Christianity in particular. I assure you that neither is the case. What is more, Campbell's insights provide a broader religious context that helps us better understand the nature of Christian beliefs, not least how the power of believing impacts human lives.

Believing is its own Reward

One of the most popular religious songs ever written is "I Believe." Actually, its "religious" overtone is more implicit than explicit, as the popularity of the Frankie Laine recording of it on the television show, "Your Hit Parade," suggested when it was released and the fact that several pop singers also recorded the song, including Elvis. Here are the lyrics:

I believe for every drop of rain that falls
A flower grows
I believe that somewhere in the darkest night
A candle glows
I believe for everyone that goes astray
Someone will come to show the way
I believe
I believe
I believe above the storm the smallest prayer
Will still be heard

---

[3]The PBS series, "Joseph Campbell and the Power of Myth," was released in 1987. It is currently available on Netflix. The transcript version, *The Power of Myth*, was published by Anchor Books, 1991.

I believe that someone in the great somewhere
Hears every word
Every time I hear a newborn baby cry
Or touch a leaf
Or see the sky
Then I know why
I believe

(Songwriters: ROGER WHITTAKER;
© Universal Music Publishing Group,
Sony/ATV Music Publishing LLC)

The popularity of the song was obviously enhanced by a tune that was and is one of those you can't stop humming to yourself once you hear it. On the surface the song seems to be about what you believe, but a closer examination reveals that it is more about the power of believing rather than the beliefs themselves. In other words, the "message" it conveys is not that you should believe everything the songs says you should believe. Instead, it's about the impact of believing things that seem like miracles or move you emotionally. Whether or not the beliefs the song includes are true is immaterial. It doesn't matter whether every raindrop makes a flower grow, a baby crying is a reminder of God, a candle is lit in every dark night, a way is shown to everyone who loses their way, or anything else. What counts is that believing these things has the power to strengthen your resolve not to let circumstances overwhelm you.

The difference is subtle, but significant. It is easy to think the impact of believing something gives validity to the belief itself, but that is not the case at all. In reality beliefs possess no power in and of themselves. They are essentially benign, having no effect on you one way or the other unless and until you begin believing them. They are like sitting in a car with the gear in neutral. You cannot move until you put it in gear. The act of believing puts the car in gear. That's when you start to move, when the beliefs begin to affect you. Understanding the powerful force believing is in human life is key to understanding the nature of beliefs themselves. This power of believing affects people's lives in good and bad ways. That impact is real whether the belief is or not. Let me illustrate.

The word *acheropite* comes from a Greek word that means "not created by human hands" and is associated with the phenomenon of Christians seeing the face of Jesus in all kinds of things such as coins, mountain sides, on the face of stones, and even in food. In 2018 a Catholic woman in Houston, Texas was interviewed on television because people started showing up at her home to see an image on the tree just outside her living room window she said was the face of Jesus. That "face of Jesus," she said, was God's message to the world that Jesus was not some place far way, but was with them here on earth. We know, of course, that if what the woman saw was the face of Jesus neither she nor anyone else would know it since no one living today has ever seen Jesus and has no idea what he looked like. That didn't matter to this woman or the people who flocked to her house to see Jesus' face in the tree. She believed she saw the face of Jesus, and those who came to see for themselves believed her.

That story draws attention to the power of believing even though the content of what is believed is suspicious at best, and at worse an absurdity. But more often than not the power of believing is seen in instances that cause us to marvel or to be grateful for the outcome. There are instances every day and throughout history where the power of believing changed a person's life, got them through a difficult situation, or empowered them to do what they could and would not have done. The life of Ida B. Wells was an inspiring example.

Theologian James Cone tells her story in his book, *The Cross and The Lynching Tree*.[4] It is a sobering book, especially for all white Americans, few of whom among us know about the history of hangings in this country. Believing in a God who knew their suffering and would ultimately redeem it was the key to the black experience in America. Ida Wells embodied what can happen when the power of believing is a driving force in life, especially believing in God's help fighting against impossible odds. She was a woman with an iron will who was determined to expose the racism behind the lynching of black men falsely accused of assaulting white women in Memphis, Tennessee. She went so far as to put her own life in danger by publicly condemning what was happening in a newspaper editorial. Later she would say that her faith in God was what gave her the courage to take a stand. She believed God was on the side of the oppressed and would show them the way to freedom. She also believed that a white Christianity

---

[4](NY: Orbis, reprint edition, 2013).

that supported racism and segregation preached a gospel "as phony as a two-dollar bill."[5]

The key to Ida Wells being able to fight against the barbarism of southern lynching of black men and women and even children was believing that God would help her prevail. It didn't matter then and it doesn't matter now whether God did in fact help her prevail. What does matter is that she believed God would and the power of her believing is what kept her going. By her own testimony she would have given up even though she knew she was right had she not believed God would help her win the fight.

That is how the power of believing can work. In her book, *The Hiding Place*,[6] Corrie ten Boom tells her inspiring story of the power of believing sustaining her after she and her sister were arrested by the Nazis for hiding Jews in their home in Holland. They were eventually sent to a concentration camp where her sister died before liberation. Corrie survived, she said, because she never stopped believing in a good God who was with them in such a horrible place. Later she described her faith as believing that there was no pit so deep that God was not deeper still.

Martin Luther King, Jr. had a similar experience he described in a sermon published in the volume, *Strength To Love*.[7] As soon as he became the leader and spokesman for the Montgomery, Alabama bus boycott, he and his family began receiving death threats on a regular basis. A late night caller who threatened them yet again upset him so much he could not go back to sleep. He said he got up, went to the kitchen, fixed a pot of coffee, sat down, and put his head in his hands, and admitted to himself that he was afraid and ready to quit. It was in that very moment he said he inwardly heard the voice of God telling him he was not alone and not to give up, to stand up for justice, to stand up for righteousness. From that moment on he never stopped believing those words he heard inwardly that terrible night. Three days later the King home was bombed. He said he received the word with surprising calm.

Of course, probably the most well-known example of the impact of what a person believes can have is Alcoholics Anonymous (AA). The second of

---

[5] loc 3755, Kindle Version.

[6] Mass Market Paperback, 1966 Edition.

[7] NY: Harper & Row, 1963, Sermon: "Our God Is Able," p. 117.

the Twelve Steps calls for the recovering alcoholic to believe in a higher power: "Came to believe that a power greater than myself could restore me to sanity." The first step is to admit you have a problem. Next is to believe a higher power can help you. The step does not specify who or what that "higher power" must be, only that working the steps means believing in a power higher than yourself that can restore you to sanity. Any recovering alcoholic will tell you that believing in a higher power is the critical step. All of them are essential, but the second step is the foundational one without which the others won't work the way they can.

That is the kind of impact believing can have. It's the power of standing firm instead of giving up, holding on instead of letting go. Whether you can prove God is present or will respond to your pleas doesn't matter. The act of believing becomes the power to redeem any moment, transcend circumstances, and change your life. Even people who are not religious can have this experience, praying as they often do when they are in trouble, as the often used phrase, "there are no atheists in fox holes," expresses.

Novelist C. J. Box captured such a moment in his book, *The Highway*.[8] Sixteen year old Gracie Sullivan and her older sister, Danielle, are being held captive by two vile sexual predators in an abandoned bomb shelter where they were being abused physically and knew they would eventually be sexually assaulted before being killed. The two men had done it before to women they had captured, raped, and killed. At their wit's end, scared to death, and not knowing what else to do, Gracie starts to pray: "God, please help us get out of here. I know we haven't paid much attention to you lately, but we really need your help."[9]

That was it. Gracie prayed because the act of praying was for her the same as the act of believing God would help her and her sister survive their ordeal. That was all that mattered at the moment. People pray because they need help and have exhausted all other resources and don't know what else to do or where else to turn. Prayer is for them a tangible way to express their belief that current circumstances will not have the last word. People of faith, little faith, and no faith pray in difficult situations because they need to cling to the hope for something better than what they are experiencing.

---

[8] St. Martin's Griffin; Reprint edition: April 16, 2019.

[9] From the audio version of the book: Macmillan Audio, Holter Graham (Narrator).

People who believe in God or don't believe in God pray. When bad happens we ask for God's help. It is the way we express hope survive the darkness and get through to the light on the other side. It asked, most people would likely not be able to tell you what they expect God to do to help them when they pray. They do so because they don't know what else to do. Praying gives them the strength to hold on and not give up. It is the belief that there is hope when nothing else suggests there is.

Praying is Believing

The subject of prayer may be the most perplexing issue people of faith face. Traditional prayers, mostly petitionary, unavoidably create an image of a God who is capricious and arbitrary, answering some, but not others. The frequent statement that God always answers prayers, we just don't know what it is all the time, is an attempt to explain the inexplicable. Equally so is insisting God is wiser than we are and knows when to answer prayers and when not to. In both instances people are speaking on behalf of God, a presumptive prerogative at best.

On the other hand, to dismiss prayer as a useless exercise is to deny the point this chapter is underscoring. It seems to me that a fresh understanding of prayer that takes it seriously while avoiding the pitfalls of petitionary prayer is to see it as a legitimate expression of the power of believing. This shifts the focus away from the need that gives rise to prayers in the first place onto the act of believing prayer represents. Praying is something people do because of a need they have instead of God needing to be nudged to pay attention to a situation requiring divine intervention.

It is not possible to control or even influence what people pray for. Earlier generations prayed for people suffering from diseases that have now been cured. Plagues that once wiped out entire European and Chinese civilizations are now controlled by knowledge about their causes (rats, fleas, prairie dogs) and the development of effective vaccinations. Influenza that still kills people yearly has effective vaccines that minimize that potential. Surgeries of every imaginable kind are performed today to save people's lives that were not possible only a few years ago, including organ transplants the church might well have labeled "of the devil" in the Middle Ages had they been possible. I have literally known people to ask for prayers because they were suffering from a headache and a cold.

The subject of petitionary prayers can trivialize praying itself, but even when petitions involve genuine needs, they get bogged down in beliefs about God that are troublesome unless the purpose of praying is understood as an expression of the power of believing. Something good happens to people who pray even when the petition "fails." People who are prayed for die. Circumstances prayed for don't change for the better. But praying never "fails" when the point is what it does for the person doing it. In short, praying is about us, not about God answering prayers. I pray for the safety of my children when they travel even though I don't believe their safety is in the hands of God. I pray for them because I need to verbalize my anxiety, worries, and fears. How my petitions impact God, or don't, is immaterial. I pray because I need to, period.

The value of this way of thinking about prayer is confirmed by modern psychology that has uncovered how transformative it can be when people tangibly express for the first time what has been residing inside their minds or hearts. It is an act of release that cannot happen any other way. The very act of saying something makes it real, which in turn brings it to life. Praying for someone you love who is ill to get better allows you to put what is inside your mind and heart into words, to give it wings, so to speak. It is called "speaking" your fears, your worries. This act can also release positive energy that has been blocked by unspoken fears and anxieties. Life has energy that works on our behalf when we get out of its way. It's another dimension of the mystery of being alive.

Praying can also do what is called "centering," a process of calming a person inwardly that allows them to shut out the noise of the world in order to focus on being present to God. Centering prayer, as it is called, is an inward turning as a way to regain balance, calm, perspective, and resolve in order to enter back into life better equipped to cope with whatever happens. Listening is a lost art that centering prayer reclaims as a key to discerning the paths we should follow and the decisions we have to make. Our world is full of noise, so much so that people openly show discomfort with any extended period of silence. The call for a moment of silence or prayer that lasts only a few seconds reveals much about the noisy lives people lead.

Personal experience has also taught me that praying means something to the person on whose behalf the praying is taking place. When my mother died, friends sent condolences that including comments that I was being remembered in their prayers. That meant a lot to me personally, though I didn't think about any effect their praying would have. It was enough to be remembered.

Because images of God matter, I have found myself deeply troubled by numerous prayer requests people make or when I hear people saying it was by God's hand that someone recovered from an illness or survived an accident. My mind immediately goes to the person who didn't recover or survive. Why didn't God answer the prayers offered on their behalf? It is only in thinking about the power of prayer as another way to talk about the power of believing that I am able to get beyond beliefs about God I find so troubling. Praying is actually a beautiful thing when understood as something for us rather than for God.

There is a song in the brilliant musical, "Les Miserables," that captures this spirit beautifully. The play is based on Victor Hugo's novel by the same name.[10] The song, entitled, "Bring Him Home," and sung by the lead character, Jean Valjean, is a prayer for the safety of a young man named Marius with whom Valjean's adopted daughter has fallen in love. The first lines are:

God on high
Hear my prayer
In my need
You have always been there

He is young
He's afraid
Let him rest
Heaven blessed.
Bring him home
Bring him home
Bring him home.

---

[10] Modern Library; 1st edition, September 5, 1992.

People need to believe in the power of believing, and praying is among the ways they express it. But the subject of the prayer is never really its point or its power. Rather, the act of praying is both the point and the power.

One further aspect of understanding praying as an expression of the power of believing is the fact that we can pray all the time. The Apostle Paul urged the Christians at Thessalonica to pray unceasingly (1 Thessalonians 5:17). Father Henri Nouwen interpreted that to mean thinking in the presence of God. Prayer, he said, was "standing in the presence of God with the mind in the heart, at that point of our being where there are no divisions or distinctions and where we are totally one," by which he meant "the center of our being.[11] Because our minds are filled with thoughts, unceasing thoughts, in fact, when we are conscious of God those unceasing thoughts become a way of praying without ceasing. "Prayer is the presentation of our thoughts," he wrote, "reflective, as well as daydreams, and night dreams, to the One who receives them, sees them in the light of unconditional love, and responds to them with divine compassion." He called this an "unceasing conversation with God."[12]

A Muslim friend understands the call to prayer in his faith tradition in a similar way. He has his phone programed to ring a bell softly five times a day as the Muslim call to prayer. One day we were together in my home when it went off. He explained that it was the call to prayer. I responded that I would be glad to wait while he went to pray. He said that would not be necessary, that in truth the call to prayer five times a day was the Muslim practice of God consciousness. Since he was conscious of God at that moment (our conversation was about God), he did not need to pray. He then told me that once he kidded with his brother-in-law who lives in Morocco where my friend is from. They were talking on the phone when his brother-in-law interrupted their conversation to say he had to go because he had just heard the call to prayer. "Ah," my friend responded, "go and pray, if you must, since you apparently have not been conscious of God as you should have been."

---

[11] *The Way of the Heart: The Spirituality of the Desert Fathers and Mothers* (HarperSan-Francisco, 1981), p. 69.

[12] "Fearless Conversation with God: Henri Nouwen on Prayer and Introspection," an interview with James Wilhoit, "The Table" https://cct.biola.edu/fearless-conversation-god-henri-nouwen-prayer-and-introspection/.

He shared this story to make the point that the call to prayer in Islam serves the purpose of reminding Muslims of the need to be conscious of God all the time. When he is, he is already praying by thinking in the presence of God and does not need to stop and pray. This leads to the conclusion that praying without ceasing is also believing without ceasing as long as you are conscious of God.

Means of Survival

This power of believing is one of the ways people get through the worst of circumstances because it keeps the hope of the future alive, so much so that it can literally save your life, as psychiatrist Victor Frankel discovered while in four different Nazi concentration camps. In his book, *Man's Search For Meaning,* he describes in compelling detail the unimaginable experience of life in the camps, including Auschwitz. The key, he observed, to surviving such evil was believing the horror would one day end. "The prisoner who had lost faith in the future — his future — was doomed," he wrote.[13]

In one passage Frankel tells the story of his senior block warden at Auschwitz, a well-known composer and librettist, who confided to him one day that he had a dream in which it was revealed that the camp would be liberated March 30, 1945. Convinced the voice in his dream was real, his friend was full of hope that liberation was coming. But as the date of liberation drew near, news from the war front was dire, making it unlikely that the man's hopes would be fulfilled. On March 29 he fell ill with a high fever and died on the thirty-first, a day after freedom was to have come. The diagnosis was that he died of typhus, but Frankel and the other prisoners knew better. "The ultimate cause of my friend's death was that the expected liberation did not come and he was severely disappointed. This suddenly lowered his body's resistance against the latent typhus infection. His faith in the future and his will to live became paralyzed and his body fell victim to illness — and thus the voice of his dream was right after all." The war and suffering was over for him.[14]

---

[13] *Man's Search For Meaning* (Boston: Beacon Press, 2005, p. 74).

[14] Ibid., p. 75.

Frankel tells other stories based on what he himself experienced and what he observed about others as a psychiatrist during those dark days in the camps to which he was taken. He survived and later resumed his psychiatric practice, using a therapeutic method he called "logotherapy" that he developed based on his camp experiences. In order for life to have meaning, he concluded, people must take "responsibility to find the right answer to its problems and to fulfill the tasks which it constantly sets for each individual."[15] A person's state of mind holds the key, especially in regard to suffering. It was not a matter of understanding suffering, but in how one bears it. Believing in the future was a necessary element in making it through suffering. Ultimately his Nazi camp experiences led Frankel to believe that "man's search for meaning is the primary motivation in his life," and, further, "that it must and can be fulfilled by him alone; only then does it achieve a significance which will satisfy his own *will* to meaning."[16] A person does not discover a meaning in life, Frankel believed. He or she makes or creates meaning in the particular circumstances he or she is facing. That is why hope is so important. To lose hope is to lose the ability to make meaning.

Prisoners who had the capacity to create an image of life after liberation, Frankel saw first-hand, were the ones who marshaled the strength to endure the suffering they were experiencing. They had no way of knowing whether what they imagined would ever come true. Frankel himself dreamed of seeing his wife, his brother, and his parents again when in truth they were already dead. The capacity to believe in a future was the critical factor in his finding meaning in each and all circumstances he faced.

The search for meaning Frankel believed was the primary human need shaped by the role the power of believing plays in our lives. Frankel saw people live and die based on their capacity to believe in a future. Those who believed they would be reunited with loved ones were more likely to survive than those who did not. Whether or not what they believed was true or even had much chance of being true did not actually matter. The power of believing was the critical factor in influencing whether some of the men he knew survived those horrible, inhumane circumstances.

---

[15] p. 77.
[16] p. 99.

This same power of believing is at work in what is known as "Play Therapy" for children traumatized by abuse and neglect. A child psychologist friend explained it to me this way:

> At this stage of development, children can harness the power of believing in ways that we, as adults, have long forgotten how to do. This can be illustrated in their belief that superheroes exist, and that these superheroes can overcome the "bad guys/gals" who hurt them and other children like them. On this same note, many children believe that they, themselves, can have "superpowers" that allow good to triumph over evil. This takes time to establish, of course, and requires the establishment of a trustworthy therapeutic relationship resulting in the felt sense of safety on which their "work" is built …. By way of the power of believing, the child slowly, but surely, heals through metaphor. To this end, it is not only the child's beliefs that lead him/her into an initial referral for Play Therapy (such as the belief that they are "bad", which often leads to engagement in negative behaviors), but also the power of their belief in POSSIBILITY which allows for their eventual "re-working" of the negative behavior-driven belief, to that of a healthier, more empowered set of beliefs naturally driven toward better functioning and growth.

You can see from all these diverse stories that the power of believing is far more significant than you might have supposed. It is easy to get focused on what someone believes that can actually be demonstrably false or quite negative, overlooking the reality that the act of believing what they believe is the key factor, whether it is a child or an adult. This should not surprise us, according to Joseph Campbell, because the power of believing is one of the enduring expressions of the power of myth in religious traditions. This is why Campbell's work sheds light on the distinction I am making between a beliefs-based Christianity and a values-based one. In order to explore what Campbell says about the power of myth, I have chosen to devote a chapter of its own to the subject at the end of which I will circle back in connecting how it intersects with the power of believing.

3

Myth and Story

Merely to mention the word "myth" when talking about Christian beliefs sets many Christians on edge. They assume you're saying that what they believe is not true, that the gospel accounts are false, written by the church to get people to believe in Jesus as the Messiah even though he wasn't. This defensive reaction is because they understand the meaning of "myth" as an imaginary story, much like a children's fairy tale, but intended for adults. Actually, myth means "a usually traditional story of ostensibly historical events that serves to unfold part of the world view of a people or explain a practice, belief, or natural phenomenon." It also means "a popular belief or tradition that has grown up around something or someone."[17]

It is these latter meanings that are the core of what Joseph Campbell had to say about the power of myth in ancient cultures and all religions. Myths, he said, were not inspiring stories about people who lived notable lives. Rather, "myth is the transcendent in relationship to the present,"[18] or "the transparent to the transcendent."[19] It's purpose is "awakening in the individual a sense of awe and mystery and gratitude for the ultimate mystery

---

[17] Merriam-Webster at merriam-webster.com.

[18] *Pathways to Bliss: Mythology and Personal Transformation* (California: New World Library, 2004), p. xvi.

[19] p. xvii.

of being."[20] The question, then, to ask about myth, Campbell said, should be about what kind of impact it has on the people who believe it. Asking if a myth is true or false is the wrong question to ask because it takes you down the wrong road in understanding its power.[21] From his perspective, the stories and myths that lie behind religious beliefs matter, not because they are historically reliability, but because those stories affect individuals and cultures. This is why Campbell had a profound appreciation for the power of myth in all the world's religions. Myth making is common because the stories people tell themselves give their lives meaning and purpose, comfort and strength. Campbell found that the power of myth not only played a decisive role in the sustainability of religions and cultures, but that neither ever existed without myth at its core. This is because myth, Campbell said, serves four functions.

The first is mystical wherein we realize the wonder of the universe, the wonder every human being is, the wonder all life is, that myth underlies all forms of existence.[22] The second function is cosmological, the dimension with which science is concerned by uncovering the shape of the universe that affirms the mystery that is endemic to it.[23] Myth's third function is sociological. Campbell said, "supporting and validating a certain social order" that is different in various places which accounts for the immense diversity of human civilizations. It is this third function that gives rise to ethical laws by which cultures, societies, and religions govern themselves.[24] The final function of myth is what he called "pedagogical," referring to the power of myths to teach people "how to live a human lifetime under any circumstances."[25]

In his study of comparative religions and cultures Campbell found common themes running through all religions, especially the hero myth found in virtually every known ancient and modern religion. Indeed, he believed

---

[20] p. 104.

[21] *Thou Art That: Transforming Religious Metaphor* (California: New World Library, 2001), pp. 1–2.

[22] *The Power of Myth*, p. 38.

[23] Ibid., 39.

[24] Ibid.

[25] Ibid.

much of religious doctrine distorted the truth "disguised for us under the figures of religion and mythology."[26] The key to it all, he said, was learning again how to read their symbolic language.[27] As such Campbell's work represents a indirect challenge to both biblical literalism and the historical critical method of study of the Bible, something that seems to have been virtually ignored.

The reason his thinking challenges both is because each in its own way diminishes the power of biblical stories to influence people across generations. Literalism seeks to historicize everything and historical criticism seeks to get behind "myths" to "real" history. Campbell called this the process of subjugating the connotative meaning of a text, that is, its spiritual significance rooted in the metaphors the Bible uses, to the denotative meaning that refers to time and space, or history.[28] "It has always puzzled me greatly," he wrote, "that the emphasis in the professional exegesis of the entire Judeo-Christian-Islamic mythology has been on the denotative rather than the connotative meaning of the metaphoric imagery that is its active language."[29]

Think for a moment about the hermeneutical or interpretative tool called "de-mythologizing" associated with the work of German theologian, Rudolph Bultmann, and his seminal book, *Theology of the New Testament: (Vol 1 & Vol 2).*[30] Even though in the 75 plus years since Bultmann's work challenged the field of New Testament studies there has been push back against his approach, demythologizing remains a fundamental principle in historical critical study, something Campbell thought was a mistake. Seeking to free the Christian gospels of the ancient world's cosmology and pre-scientific world view, that is, to demythologize biblical stories and texts, was precisely the wrong thing to do, not because the Bible does not contain myths, but because it does.

In a different way, the Jesus Seminar that once stirred up controversy over the historical unreliability of what the gospel accounts say about Jesus

---

[26] *The Hero With A Thousand Faces* (New World Library; Third edition, 2008), p. xii.

[27] Ibid.

[28] *Thou Art That* (California: New World Library, 2001), p. 7.

[29] Ibid.

[30] (New York: Charles Scribner's, 1951); Volume 2 was published in 1955.

made the same mistake by trying to find the historical Jesus and the few things he actually said. Campbell would say that neither historical credibility nor demythologizing addressed the reason for the Bible in the first place. Mythology is not extraneous to the biblical message, but core to it because stories were the means by which biblical writers passed on their beliefs to future generations. Exorcising mythical material from biblical stories and texts or exposing their historical unreliability does not enable us to understand them better. Quite the opposite. It robs us of seeing the truth about life and God and ourselves conveyed in the material as we have it, and how it functioned in the life of those who first told the stories.

Telling myths, Campbell said, is how all people in all times try to connect with the transcendent. Myths, he said, "are the clues to the spiritual potentialities of the human life."[31] Moreover, they serve as spiritual bridges between the transcendent or God and the present, pointing to what is real, yet indescribable."[32] That is why myth is not history, a common mistake he said religions make because they interpret "mythological symbols as if they were references to historical facts…[a] problem particularly crucial in our [religious] tradition in the West, where the whole emphasis has been in the historicity of the events on which our churches are supposed to have been founded."[33] Put another way, Campbell said that mythology is intended to "arouse in the mind a sense of awe," and in this way it serves its essentially religious function which he described as "mystical," or "the discovery and recognition of the dimension of the mystery of being.[34]

I think Campbell's work on the power of myth offers Christians insight into the power of biblical stories that may or may not have historical grounding, but still convey truth. In Chapter 10 I will discuss the meaning of "story" in detail. For now I want to say that the power of biblical stories lies precisely where Campbell said the power of myth does—in the impact those stories have had and continue to have on people. This is not to say that biblical stories are untrue. Rather, it is to say that the historical grounding of those stories is immaterial to the power of the stories themselves. In short, biblical stories speak truth that transcends history because their intent is not

---

[31] *The Power of Myth*, p. 5.

[32] *Pathways To Bliss*, pp. xvi–xvii.

[33] Ibid., p. 21.

[34] *Thou Art That*, p. 3.

historical, but theological, to connect people to God. Campbell's work frees religion from living in the shadow of the enlightenment thinking that values scientific reasoning above everything else. Indeed, he warned of the seduction of faith weighed down by reason and logic to the extreme and, thus diminishing the emotive side of faith.

Campbell's insights bring to mind old gospel hymns I grew up singing. The theology in them is not what I believe today, but I still love singing them. The old African American spiritual, "Were You There," holds the emotional impact for me now that it always has. The appeal of old hymns and spirituals is emotional, not intellectual, connecting me and others to something beyond ourselves in spite of the actual theology of those songs. Campbell would say that is the power of myth at work. I would say it is how biblical stories have become the foundation for the power of believing at work among Christians as these old gospel hymns express the emotional bond biblical stories have created in us. Here is another illustration of this point.

I first began writing this book during Advent season, a curious convergence of timing since I had just finished reading through Campbell's work and could see what he was saying in the season all Christians seem to relish. Each week of Advent churches read a portion of the story of the birth of Jesus, beginning with an angel telling Mary she is "with child" not of human origin, but of God, about shepherds being greeted by angels telling them of the good news that the birth has taken place, about "wise men" travelling from the east to Jerusalem and then on to Bethlehem to pay homage to this special child, and Mary and Joseph making an escape to Egypt when the Roman Emperor seeks to find the babe to kill him. For generations carols telling the various aspects of this story have been sung in churches around the world, carols so familiar that Christians sing the words by memory. This is the church's story called "Christmas," and I love to read and tell it like most other Christians.

Told on the basis of historical realities, however, the Christmas story completely loses its power as story. Critical study of the Bible says there was no virgin, that the whole thing was a misunderstanding based on a mistranslation of Isaiah 7:14 on which it is based. Matthew and Luke who tell the birth stories about Jesus used the Greek translation of the Old Testament called the Septuagint that mistakenly used the word "virgin" when Isaiah 7:14 actually says in Hebrew "young maiden or woman": "Therefore the

Lord himself will give you a sign. Look, the young woman is with child and shall bear a son, and shall name him Immanuel." The Hebrew word "almah" can mean "virgin," but also means "young woman of marriageable age or maid or newly married." The fact that there is another Hebrew word for virgin, "*bethulah*," that could have also been used in the text strongly suggests the intent of the original text was "young maiden," not "virgin."

What is more, we know the church set the date of Christmas because of the pagan celebration of the winter solstice without thinking about the problem that time of the year raised regarding shepherds taking sheep to the fields in the dead of winter. The story of the Wise Men was most assuredly a later addition to the story. Finally, only two of the four gospels include the birth of Jesus narrative, and even those two (Matthew and Luke) couldn't get their stories straight. All in all, a historical study of the Advent and Christmas story essentially destroys it by taking away all the mythology attached to it that allows the story of Jesus' birth to serve its purpose in Christian tradition. In short, it is unlikely we would have the Advent/Christmas seasons as we do today had the demythologized (historical critical analysis) story of Jesus' birth been all the church had. Most people need to have something more to hold on to, and the stories in the Bible do that for them just as they are written and regardless of whether or not they are true.

The power of believing is an awesome thing. Sometimes we know deep down that what we believe is not or may not be true, but it doesn't matter. When my family gathers for Thanksgiving Dinner we end up telling family stories. They may contain a kernel of truth, but the family knows they are embellished, expanded, and revised every time they are told, and we don't care. We laugh or cry anyway because all that matters is that we tell the story and at the moment of telling it gives us identity and hope, a feeling of connectedness to one another, and sometimes a sense of being connected to God. None of that makes the story true, which is why we don't focus on the details. The story is sufficient just as it is.

Doubt and the Power of Believing

As awesome as the power of believing can be, doubt remains a significant factor in the world of faith, not as a stumbling block, but as a precaution that can serve you well. One of the most fascinating stories in the Bible about doubt involves the disciple, Thomas, who is told by the other disciples that Jesus has been raised from the dead. Thomas responds by saying he will believe it when he sees it. "Unless I see the mark of the nails in his hands, and put my finger in the mark of the nails and my hand in his side, I will not believe" (John 20:25) is what he said to them.

A week later Thomas got his wish. Jesus came to the disciples once again as they were gathered in "the house." The story doesn't tell us why Jesus spoke to Thomas as he did, but in the story he says to him, "Put your finger here and see my hands. Reach out your hand and put it in my side. Do not doubt but believe" (John 20:26-27). That was all Thomas needed. He believed, and in believing he became an effective Christian missionary, establishing the first church in Babylon or modern-day Iraq, throughout Mesopotamia, and as far as India. Thomas is known for his doubting, but in truth what he wanted was some evidence that gave credibility to the claims the other disciples were making.

As I have underscored several times, the power of believing does not depend on what you believe being true. Believing it is true is enough. But Thomas stood at the beginning of the birth of Christianity. Jesus being alive after witnessing his crucifixion was not something he was about to believe without a reason, not least because the first telling of a story cannot be demonstrably false without raising moral and ethical questions about its telling. This is always true at the beginning of a story. Someone has to be the teller who has some reason to tell it, and in this instance the story involved a dead man being alive again. Thomas was not going to be party to an outright falsehood. He needed to be convinced that believing Jesus was alive made sense. We know he eventually found what he needed.

The key point I take away from the Thomas story that relates to what we are discussing is that it affirms that the power of believing is not altered by honoring your doubts. That is how you maintain your personal integrity without giving up the act of believing itself. It is unfortunate, that the church has used "doubting Thomas" in a pejorative way to illustrate the temptations doubt presents. Doubts are not temptations. They are questions that come into your mind as a thinking person. Robots don't have doubts. People do. One meaning of the word "skepticism" is "the method of suspended judgment." That can be a very good thing before passing judgment or drawing a conclusion. Eventually to believe something will require you to take a "leap of faith."

One reason the issue of doubt is important is because in my own experience I am never without an element of doubt about matters of faith. If faith means having no doubts, I don't qualify. But that is a false requirement. In truth, I think it shows a strength of faith that you can believe even though you have doubts. The power of believing is not about eliminating doubts. It is about believing "in spite of" them, sometimes intensified by feelings of God being absent rather than present that can descend on anyone, even one as saintly as Mother Teresa of Calcutta.

No one in the 20th century was more admired than Mother Teresa because of her compassionate work with India's poorest of the poor. Her name would be at the top of anyone's list of women who were examples of great faith. British journalist Malcolm Muggeridge's book about her was appropriately entitled, *Something Beautiful for God*.[35] She was declared a saint by the Catholic Church in 2003 and no one deserved it more. Yet, by her own confession, she lived without feeling like God was with her. She relied on her faith, but inwardly suffered from a relentless sense of loneliness she attributed to the absence of God.

In her book, *Mother Teresa: Come Be My Light—The Private Writings of the Saint of Calcutta*, a posthumously published collection of her letters to her spiritual directors and superiors written over many years, she wrote of living with the "companion of darkness,"[36] similar to the state of "the dark night of the soul" about which St. John of the Cross wrote in describing the sense of the absence of God people of faith often experience.[37] Mother Teresa wrote of loneliness so intense that at one point she felt like she was a hypocrite for having so many doubts about her own faithfulness. "Darkness," she wrote to Father Joseph Neuner, "is such that I really do not see—neither with my mind nor with my reason—the place of God in

---

[35] HarperOne; Reprint edition (August 26, 2003).

[36] *Come Be My Light* (NY: Doubleday, 2007), p. 20.

[37] St. John of the Cross, *Dark Night of the Soul* (CreateSpace Independent Publishing Platform, January 24, 2019).

my soul is blank—There is no God in me—when the pain of longing is so great—I just long & long for God … The torture and pain I can't explain."[38]

She frequently asked privately for prayers as she suffered with "excruciating inner pain," writing: "Please pray for me, that it may please God to lift this darkness from my soul for only a few days. For sometimes the agony of desolation is so great and at the same time the longing for the Absent One so deep, that the only prayer which I can still say is—Sacred Heart of Jesus I trust in Thee—I will satiate Thy thirst for souls."[39] And yet, she believed in God and the power of that believing enabled her to leave the safety and relative comfort of leading a school for girls for a ministry whose simple purpose was to ensure that the forgotten people of India living on the street knew before they died that they were loved. That decision led to the worldwide ministry today known as the Missionaries of Charity.

Obviously, faith and struggle exist in the same room, in the same mind, in the same heart, in the same life, in the same good and beautiful life as the one Mother Teresa lived. If it was true for her, it can be true for all of us.

---

[38] *Come Be My Light*, p. 1–2 (letter to Father John Neuner).

[39] p. 165 (letter to Archbishop Ferdinand Perier of Calcutta).

4

Excess Baggage

One of the significant historical statements of my own denomination that speaks to the discussion we are having says: "In Essentials Unity, In Non-Essentials Liberty, In All Things Charity." It expressed the aspirations of a small group of Christians in the early 1800s who had grown weary of conflicts and divisions among Christians. As it turned out, though, they were unable to live up to their ideals as they struggled to agree on "essentials" and "non-essentials." That led to less than charitable attitudes toward one another.

Christians are very good at naming ideals, but less so in living up to them. I suppose that is true with any religion that defines itself by right beliefs. The victors write the history, and therein lies the rub. When Christians have formed a group, it has usually been the result of splitting off from a previous group whose beliefs the breakaways could no longer accept. They would then postulate their beliefs and, wouldn't you know, at some point they would undergo the same kind of split for the same reasons that led them to form their own group. The Catholic Church has done amazingly well in holding things together, but only by the force of history and tradition, while allowing more freedom of expression through monastic orders whose focus was and is on mission, not beliefs. Protestants, on the other hand, have determinedly persisted in gathering around a set of beliefs that never satisfy everyone and, thus, one group ends up spawning another group.

I am not so presumptuous as to think I have come upon a solution to this problem, but I do want to suggest a way forward if you are unable to believe the things you were taught to believe or the things you think you should believe to be a Christian. There is, I believe, only one thing that should be considered essential for anyone wanting to be Christian. It is having a genuine and unequivocal desire to live your life the way Jesus lived his. This is what I think Jesus himself said when he called his disciples. He simply said, "Follow me." That is what living your life as Jesus lived his means—following the values he lived and taught.

Jean Vanier, the founder of L'Arche, which are live-in communities around the world for severely physically and mentally handicapped persons and their caregivers, described his decision to leave the British military with the simple words, "I felt called by Jesus." He continued, "to take another path … I left the Navy and did a doctorate in philosophy at the University of Paris, started teaching … and then through a priest-friend I had the good fortune of meeting people with mental disabilities."[40] It was then that he discovered welcoming people with mental and physical disabilities into his life and his home was what following Jesus meant in his life. Jean Vanier was a living reminder of how redemptive being in the world in a particular way can be for the person and for others. This it seems to me is the one essential for being Christian—a way of life, being in the world in a way that is redemptive by the power of unconditional love.

Early in ministry I read a book by a Catholic Priest in which he discussed the problem of the church's pedestalization of Jesus that had made him inaccessible for ordinary people. The singular statement he made that I remember even to this day and strikes me as being as true as it was when I first read it was his saying that the challenge Christians face is to live our lives as authentically as Jesus lived his.[41] That is what Christianity being a lifestyle means, taking the values Jesus lived seriously enough to incorporate them into the way you live, a life that is more demanding than believing what the church says are the right things you should believe. The desire to live this way is the core of Christianity. It's the point of being a Christian. You can be

---

[40] Jean Vanier, From *Brokenness To Community* (NY: Paulist Press, 1992), p. 11. (My wife and I heard him described his experience in a lecture at Augsburg College, Minneapolis, MN, in 2006).

[41] Unfortunately, I failed to keep the book. An extensive search has yet to yield any reference to it.

just as religious if you follow the teachings of the Torah, Mohammed, the Buddha, or someone else. Choosing to be Christian means following the teachings of Jesus, choosing to live a lifestyle based on the values he lived and taught.

Implicit in the desire to follow Jesus is the choice to believe in God. something most people take for granted. I raise it here to draw attention to the important role that choice plays, a choice that cannot be proven true or false. God is not a fact. God is the name we give to what we call "the transcendent." When you speak of God, you are not expressing what you know to be true, only what you know you believe is true. Someone else may not make that choice, and neither of you can prove yourself right and the other wrong. What you can be sure of, however, is that your choice has enormous consequences. Once you believe in God I think it is fair to say that your life is no longer your own. Instead, you have chosen to make doing the will of God a basic value in and for your life. That means you have voluntarily put yourself in the role of holding yourself accountable to a different standard of living.

In addition, of equal importance is how you think about God, that is, what image of God you are carrying around. Not all "gods" are the same. Here is where the way Jesus talked about God—directly and indirectly— becomes helpful, in part because the Bible contains more than one image of God, often in marked contrast one from the other. The image of God in the book of Deuteronomy, for example, is quite different from the image found in the Book of Job. Not only do the two images contradict one another, a close examination of both books strongly suggests Job was written with the intention of challenging Deuteronomy.

Deuteronomy is organized around five "sermons" Moses preaches to the Hebrew people just before they enter the Promised Land. There is one theme running through all five "sermons." If you are good, God will bless you. If you are bad, God will curse you. It is called the Deuteronomic ethic of blessings and curses. "Hear therefore, O Israel, and observe them [commandment, statutes, ordinances] diligently, so that it may go well with you" (Deuteronomy 6:3). This theme runs throughout the book and reflects a common image of God in the Bible as rewarding obedience and punishing disobedience. It is an image that lies at the root of the Christian belief that God will judge all of us when we die and either welcome us into heaven or send us to hell based on how obedient or disobedient we have been.

Deuteronomy lies at the heart of the Torah and shaped Israel's image of God to the point where they went another step and inverted the ethic of blessings and curses. If God blesses people who are good and curses people who are bad, then it must be equally the case that if someone is suffering, God must be punishing them. If they are enjoying success, God must be rewarding them. In a real sense, the inverted Deuteronomic ethic became a tool for identifying who was obeying the Torah commandment and who wasn't. It shows itself today when people determine that God is blessing the life of a person who is very successful and punishing someone who has lost everything. I have heard preachers say the same thing about churches, theirs in particular. If it is growing, then "we must be doing something right."

The image of God in the Book of Job is the opposite of what Deuteronomy says about God. Job is a righteous man who honors God while experiencing untold suffering inflicted on him by the angel Satan who tells God that Job is righteous only because his life is good. "The Satan" (the term used in the text) makes a wager with God that Job will turn on a dime once bad things start happening to this good man. He didn't, but along the way God and Job have a debate about the sovereignty of God as Job challenges God's actions toward him. In the end, Job's life is restored fully to overflowing and his faithfulness to God is vindicated.

The story is, of course, a parable whose setting is established by the wager between God and the Satan. A literal reading of the story destroys the theological point by painting an image of God as One willing to use human beings as a pawn to win the argument. Read for the metaphor it is, the story makes the case against the Deuteronomic ethic by rejecting an inversion of it represented by Eliphaz, Teman, and Naamathite, the three friends of Job who visit him begging him to confess his sins they are sure he committed because of his suffering. Had he not committed them he would not be suffering such punishment from God. Job rejects the argument his friends make because he knows it is untrue. That is the core message of the story. God does not reward and punish people based on what they do, wrong or right.

Jesus also rejected the Deuteronomic ethic, especially in its inverted form. His disciples once asked him whether a man or his parents sinned since he was born blind. Jesus answered them that neither did, but his blindness would be an occasion to teach them the ways of God that were light, not darkness (John 9:1-5). Moreover, God is described as love and that all who abide in God abide in love (1 John 4:16). A God who punishes and rewards according to obedience is not a God of love, though I have met more than a few Christians who try to make themselves believe the two images are consistent. They are not, any more than Deuteronomy and the Book of Job are.

Images of God matter to people of faith because they influence how we live, how we see life as a whole. No image captures God fully. The question is which one leads us to believe God can be trusted with our devotion expressed in a commitment to live the way Jesus lived, loving the way he loved. More than that, there is an incredible freedom that goes with letting go of all the things you have been told to believe about God because it makes space for you to work at being a living reminder of what Jesus said and did. A beliefs-based faith doesn't give you that space. Once you claim that space for yourself, you will immediately see that everything the church says about Jesus is an "add-on," a non-essential, to being a Christian.

I know this to be the case in part because I was raised as a Christian in a non-creedal tradition. The founders of my denomination were Scottish Presbyterians so they knew the creeds well, but chose not to use them because in their experience they ended up dividing people instead of uniting them. Even if I had been schooled in creedal Christianity, though, I could not affirm what they say, though I have no trouble repeating them as an act of worship in the name of ritual. Walk with me through the Nicene Creed, the first of the church's creeds written in 325 C.E., to see why I say that.

We believe in one God,
the Father, the Almighty,
maker of heaven and earth,
of all that is, seen and unseen.

We believe in one Lord, Jesus Christ,
the only Son of God,
eternally begotten of the Father,
God from God, Light from Light,
true God from true God,
begotten, not made,
of one Being with the Father.

Through him all things were made.
For us and for our salvation
he came down from heaven:
by the power of the Holy Spirit
he became incarnate from the Virgin Mary,
and was made man.
For our sake he was crucified under Pontius Pilate;
he suffered death and was buried.
On the third day he rose again
in accordance with the Scriptures;
he ascended into heaven
and is seated at the right hand of the Father.
He will come again in glory to judge the living and the dead,
and his kingdom will have no end.

We believe in the Holy Spirit, the Lord, the giver of life,
who proceeds from the Father and the Son.
With the Father and the Son he is worshiped and glorified.
He has spoken through the Prophets.
We believe in one holy catholic and apostolic Church.
We acknowledge one baptism for the forgiveness of sins.
We look for the resurrection of the dead,
and the life of the world to come. Amen.

While poetic, the creed speaks of non-essential Christian beliefs. The first stanza presents an image of God as the creator of all things, a logical belief for those who believe God is real. But the next stanza which is the core of the creedal statement articulates beliefs about Jesus many Christians reject as essential to their faith. Part of the reason is that the language appears to say something when in fact it doesn't. What does it mean to say Jesus is "one Lord ... the only Son of God, eternally begotten of the Father, God from God, Light from Light, true God from true God, begotten, not made, of one Being with the Father?" To say Jesus is "God from God" may mean he is God, but what does it mean to say a man is God, and, further, how could any Jew at the time of Jesus have believed such a thing when it violates the monotheistic foundation of Judaism? Is this similar to Moses asking who God is and the response is, "I am who I am" (Exodus 3:14)?

When the creed declares that Jesus came down from heaven, does that mean heaven is up? And when the Holy Spirit impregnated Mary, is that like virgin birth stories in other religions? Regarding the crucifixion, you can believe Jesus died for your sake, meaning the events were controlled by God who sent Jesus down from heaven to die to relieve you of the responsibility for your sins, but you can also understand his death in other ways as theologians have since the beginning of Christianity. The "ascended into heaven" is a problem, too, since it underscores what we know is not true, that heaven is up, or that the universe has a known end. The creed then ends by asserting that Jesus will return to judge the living and the dead.

For some Christians, even many, believing what the creed says is meaningful and important. For Christians like me, it is neither. Given the subjective nature of beliefs, is it wise or appropriate for the church to have converted statements like this into tests of faith that have only served to divide Christians? My answer is no, which is why I argue for all belief statements regarding the nature of Jesus to be labeled "non-essentials." Too much harm has been done calling them "essentials," including the church using fear as a tool of religious coercion.

Fearful Faith

When my brothers and I were kids, my oldest brother moved into his own bedroom after my parents divided our already small dining room for him to have his own space. My middle brother and I were left sharing a bedroom. I still remember nights when I would awaken and immediately look over to see if my brother was still there. After all, I believed what I had been taught by my church, that Jesus would one day return like a thief in the night and take real Christians back to heaven and leave the rest behind. I was just checking to make sure I had not been among the latter.

Not all beliefs-based faith instills that kind of fear in people, but much does and when it does it is a form of Christianity that I believe does more harm than good. One reason is that it contradicts love rather than expressing it. The writer of the first letter of John knew this, writing, "There is no fear in love, but perfect love casts out fear; for fear has to do with punishment, and whoever fears has not reached perfection in love" (1 John 4:18).

Fearful faith plays mental gymnastics with itself in juxtaposing its talk of God's love with its equal emphasis on God's judgment. It may say divine punishment is an expression of God's justice as if that makes what they are saying more positive, but it doesn't. God as love and God as judge or punisher are incompatible images of God.

Much of this goes back to the Book of Deuteronomy, as I have previously suggested. The call to obedience in Deuteronomy is interpreted by the church's institutional Christianity as a call to right beliefs. Obeying God means believing in Jesus as the church articulates those beliefs, whether through creeds, doctrines, or appeals to the authority of scripture. The original warning to the people of Israel was about idolatry, running after other gods in a polytheistic culture. Belief-based faith interprets that as a warning against believing things the church has declared wrong or heretical based on church authority in Catholicism and scripture in Protestantism. The claims in both traditions rest on an image of God as Judge and Executioner that I find unappealing. Nothing about God as One who punishes sinners makes me want to believe in God, and everything about it offends my sense of decency. Fearing God is to my mind the equivalent of fearing my parents. When I was a child I feared being punished, but when I became an adult I put away that kind of childish thinking.

I have not found a satisfactory way to reconcile the claim that God is love with an image of God who is ready to hand out blessings and curses. A message that tells me to live a good life and to do what is right so as to avoid punishment does not strike me as "good news." That is the kind of Christianity I learned as a child, but it is not the kind of Christianity I have as an adult. Fear is the tool of Christianity that treats adult Christians as perpetual children who need the threat of punishment to believe and to do what is right.

I think fear lies at the heart of a beliefs-based Christianity that judges people based on their sexual orientation and gender, just as it was with discrimination based on race. The most obvious example of this kind of fear-based judgmentalism was the argument that has been proven empirically false that gay marriage would undermine traditional marriage. There was no rhyme or reason to that argument, which is why we know it was based on fear that itself was based on ignorance. No one could explain how a gay couple being married would pose a threat to heterosexual marriage, but that didn't matter because a fearful faith needs no reason to exist. It thrives on ignorance, on no one challenging the intellectual basis for its claims. That is why the argument quietly went away once gay marriage in America was declared a constitutional right. The divorce rate among heterosexuals has not skyrocketed since, nor has there been a precipitance drop in the number of heterosexual marriages.

The connection between fear and a beliefs-based Christianity is easy to see if you understand the nature of beliefs as I discussed early on in the book. People's passion is attached to the beliefs they hold, religious and non-religious alike, because those beliefs have to do with ultimate matters—life, death, God, eternity, judgment. What is more, everybody likes to be right about what they believe, and a beliefs-based Christianity appeals to that need. When a belief held with such passion is challenged, you become defensive because your sense of self is caught up in being right. Uncertainty creates a sense of fear that you could be wrong, and if wrong on one thing, perhaps wrong on other things. The alternative is to refuse to consider being wrong and fight to the death in defending what you believe as those do who reject scientific evidence that shows the genetic influence on sexual orientation. The need to have right beliefs has instilled too much fear in them to be open to changing their attitude.

Fearing the judgment of God is without question a theme in the entire Bible, but in most instances the meaning is not "fear" per se, but reverence or awe. In the instances that texts do mean "fear," as in being afraid of, they reflect an ancient view of God other passages in scripture, including the words of Jesus, contradict. The Apostle Paul offered a different way of thinking about divine judgment that mitigates against fearing God when he wrote: "Do not be deceived; God is not mocked, for you reap whatever you sow" (Galatians 6:7). Judgment is what we bring on ourselves, not by wrong beliefs, but by wrong actions. Thus, Paul continued, "If you sow to your own flesh, you will reap corruption from the flesh; but if you sow to the Spirit, you will reap eternal life from the Spirit. So let us not grow weary in doing what is right, for we will reap at harvest time, if we do not give up. So then, whenever we have an opportunity, let us work for the good of all, and especially for those of the family of faith" (6:8-10).

What I think Paul is saying is that there are consequences to our words and actions, none of which are God's punishment. Instead, they are what we bring on ourselves and at the same time harm we cause to others. It may be that attributing to God the bad things that happen in life relieves us individually and as a society from self-examination. History shows that human beings have an endless capacity for doing bad things, matched only by our capacity to do good. It's called free will, and Paul chose to say it rather than to blame God. Indirectly he identified the reason why living by the values Jesus lived and taught is essential for all Christians. That is the subject to which we now turn our attention.

5

A Faith of Values

E arlier I made reference to the difference between being **a** Christian and being Christian. It is such an obvious distinction that it is an enigma why it has not been attended to more seriously in Christian teaching. Quite simply, being a Christian is about beliefs while being Christian is about living by the values of Jesus, or, as the Apostle Paul put it, living a life that is well-pleasing to God (Romans 12:2). That kind of life is not about having right beliefs, but about right values, values that are consistent with what we know about the will of God. This is what Jesus himself said: "Not everyone who says to me, 'Lord, Lord,' will enter the kingdom of heaven, but only the one who does the will of my Father in heaven" (Matthew 7:21).

Those words are not a call to right beliefs. They are a call to right *living*. Richard Rohr puts it this way:

> Christianity is a lifestyle—a way of being in the world that is simple, non-violent, shared, and loving. However, we made it into an established "religion" (and all that goes with that) and avoided the lifestyle change itself. One could be warlike, greedy, racist, selfish, and vain in most of Christian history, and still believe that Jesus is one's "personal Lord and Savior" … The world has no time for such silliness anymore. The suffering on earth is too great.[42]

---

[42] (https://www.inspiringquotes.us/author/5872-richard-rohr/about-christianity)

This seems to me to be what Jesus taught. His call was to a particular way of living in the world that identifies everyone who follows him as a person committed to putting the will of God first in their lives. Being Christian is more than having beliefs, even right beliefs. It goes the next step and embodies values that reflect the will of God as best we can know it. Being Christian requires a commitment to being in the world in a particular way. This is the beauty of Christianity, the lifestyle it calls you to live. And when you respond to that call, you will never again have anxiety about whether or not your life matters, because your life will be spent making the world better.

A clergy friend of mine who recently lost his battle with cancer was a living reminder of this truth. He had been a conscientious objector during the Vietnam War, serving an alternative service for two years at Boston Children's Hospital. His entire ministry was a reasoned voice for peace and justice, serving only four churches during all his years as a pastor with distinction and honor. Known for his quiet manner, he was universally remembered as a man who put God first in his life as an advocate for the powerless and voiceless wherever he served. In all the remembrances that poured in after his death, not one said anything about what he believed. All of them spoke with admiration about what he did, in many instances, what he had done for the person who was now mourning his death.

This good friend understood the difference between being a Christian and being Christian. He let his life speak of what he believed and believed in. The words he most often used were to be found in the hundreds of songs he wrote and sang in churches everywhere. What mattered to him was living a life that showed his convictions, and that is exactly how all of us who knew and loved him will remember him, a man of God whose life inspired others to be and do better.

Jesus Values

How did my friend and colleague know how to live the way he did? He knew the life and teachings of Jesus and the values that should define what it means to be Christian. I think it will help you see that clearly if I walk you through the heart of what Jesus said as found in the gospels to show you why I think the way to a joyful faith is to attend more to values than to beliefs. Jesus said it himself quite clearly and that is the place to start.

At the end of the Sermon on the Mount he said that calling him "Lord" mattered far less than doing the will of God: "Not everyone who says to me, "Lord, Lord", will enter the kingdom of heaven, but only one who does the will of my Father in heaven" (Matthew 7:21). Following him means doing what is right, living right, being a good neighbor to one another. Beliefs contribute to doing what is right by shaping attitudes that strengthen the commitment to the basic values Jesus taught and lived, but values must be our first concern.

Consider the Sermon on the Mount which is the largest single collection of the teachings of Jesus we find in the New Testament. It says virtually nothing about beliefs. Instead, the Sermon is focused almost exclusively on values, as a careful reading of it shows, beginning with the Beatitudes (Matthew 5:3-11).

Blessed are the poor in spirit, for theirs is the kingdom of heaven.
Blessed are those who mourn, for they will be comforted.
Blessed are the meek, for they will inherit the earth.
Blessed are those who hunger and thirst for righteousness, for they will be filled.
Blessed are the merciful, for they will receive mercy.
Blessed are the pure in heart, for they will see God.
Blessed are the peacemakers, for they will be called children of God.
Blessed are those who are persecuted for righteousness' sake, for theirs is the kingdom of heaven.
Blessed are you when people revile you and persecute you and utter all kinds of evil against you falsely on my account.

Being "poor in spirit" is a call to humility, a value. Comforting people who are mourning is a value. To "hunger for righteousness" means seeking justice and showing mercy to others is a value. Being pure in heart, avoiding duplicity, are values. Being a peacemaker is a value. Even being willing to endure persecution for the sake of doing what is right, even when you know people will speak against you or about you in a negative way, is a value. These are the qualities that make for Christian living, that define Christian discipleship, which are about values that reveal loyalty to God. But that is only the beginning of the Sermon. Here are other values Jesus highlighted:

> You have heard that it was said to those of ancient times, "You shall not murder"; and "whoever murders shall be liable to judgment." But I say to you that if you are angry with a brother or sister, you will be liable to judgment.

> You have heard that it was said, "You shall not commit adultery." But I say to you that everyone who looks at a woman with lust has already committed adultery with her in his heart.

> Again, you have heard that it was said to those of ancient times, "You shall not swear falsely, but carry out the vows you have made to the Lord."

> You have heard that it was said, "An eye for an eye and a tooth for a tooth." But I say to you, Do not resist an evildoer. But if anyone strikes you on the right cheek, turn the other also; and if anyone wants to sue you and take your coat, give your cloak as well; and if anyone forces you to go one mile, go also the second mile. Give to everyone who begs from you, and do not refuse anyone who wants to borrow from you.

> You have heard that it was said, "You shall love your neighbor and hate your enemy." But I say to you, Love your enemies and pray for those who persecute you.

> In everything do to others as you would have them do to you; for this is the law and the prophets.

These texts fit the larger core message of Jesus that what matters most for those who follow him is "doing" what God wants them to do, not calling him "Lord, Lord" (Matthew 7:21). Combined with the challenge of Jesus at the end of the Sermon to live by the values he named, it seems clear to me that church teaching misses the essence of the Sermon on the Mount by highlighting beliefs instead of values. Jesus says nothing in the Sermon about what you have to believe to be Christian. His focus, instead, is on how to live the kind of life that identifies you with him, a life that defines being Christian over being **a** Christian consumed with right beliefs. Values place faith on a solid foundation as if it stands on rock rather than shifting sand.

Critics of what I am saying will ask: "What about Jesus's words, 'I am the way, and the truth, and the life. No one comes to the Father except through me' (John 14:6)?" These words of Jesus, says the church, confirm that Jesus is the only means of salvation (going to "heaven"), and that the way to be with Jesus is to believe in him as the Son of God. But is that what this text really says? Allow me a bit of a sidebar to suggest that this traditional interpretation may not be at all what Jesus was saying.

First of all, let's put the verse in context. The entire passage in which it appears reads as follows:

> Do not let your hearts be troubled. Believe in God, believe also in me. In my Father's house there are many dwelling places. If it were not so, would I have told you that I go to prepare a place for you? And if I go and prepare a place for you, I will come again and will take you to myself, so that where I am, there you may be also. And you know the way to the place where I am going.

> Thomas said to him, "Lord, we do not know where you are going. How can we know the way?"

> Jesus said to him, "I am the way, and the truth, and the life. No one comes to the Father except through me. If you know me, you will know my Father also. From now on you do know him and have seen him."

> Philip said to him, "Lord, show us the Father, and we will be satisfied."

> Jesus said to him, "Have I been with you all this time, Philip, and you still do not know me? Whoever has seen me has seen the Father. How can you say, 'Show us the Father'? Do you not believe that I am in the Father and the Father is in me? The words that I say to you I do not speak on my own; but the Father who dwells in me does his works. Believe me that I am in the Father and the Father is in me; but if you do not, then believe me because of the works themselves. Very truly, I tell you, the one who believes in me will also do the works that I do and, in fact, will do greater

works than these, because I am going to the Father. I will do whatever you ask in my name, so that the Father may be glorified in the Son. If in my name you ask me for anything, I will do it." (John 14:1-14)

This text is a beautiful example of Jesus speaking metaphorically to convey his message. He speaks, for example, of "house" or mansion as translated into English (KJV used "mansion," NRSV uses "house"). Both words refer to a dwelling or building, but in Greek (in which the text was written) the word "house" often means household, family, or lineage. Because the family was at the core of Jewish life, "household" or "family" is more likely what Jesus was talking about. Thus, the text should read something like, "In my Father's family or household are many dwelling places." The sentence is a repetitive statement because "household" or "family" carries the meaning of a "dwelling place" or "a staying." In other words, all these words used by Jesus are saying the same thing to convey metaphorically the image of God's family being large enough for anyone and everyone. That is a meaning literalism cannot get you to because you are caught up in concretizing "house" and "dwelling place" or "rooms" being literal places we possess as homes.

The next statement Jesus makes reinforces this when he talks about going to prepare a "place" for his disciples. As we noted with the Nicene Creed, if Jesus is saying that "heaven" is a "place" he is going ahead of the disciples, that makes no sense in a 21st century world. In the first century, however, it did. The disciples not only believed in "heaven," they believed it was "up." If Jesus was speaking literally, he would be reflecting a first-century worldview that believed in a three-story universe where "heaven" was up, "hell" was down or below, i.e., in the underworld, and "earth" was in-between, Read this way Jesus would literally be saying that he was going "up" to heaven to get things ready for the disciples to come "up" with him.

How do we understand these words when we know there is no place "up" in the universe? The known universe is infinite, which means "up" is infinite, that is, without end. Moreover, there are no "places" in the universe because time and space are meaningless concepts in infinity. If "heaven" were a "place," then God would by definition be limited to time and space. But, then, God would not be God if that were true. God cannot be here and not there since our faith says that God is everywhere. As you can see, literalism leads to a dead-end in trying to understand what Jesus was saying in this text.

A more helpful way is to see the exchange between Jesus and Thomas as a key to this passage. Thomas verbalizes the confusion Jesus' words have created in the minds of the disciples when he says, "We don't know where you are going so how can we know the way to get there?" The answer Jesus gives is simple and direct. His way, his truth, and the life he was living is the path to follow. Anyone who does that will be where Jesus is going, which is in the presence of God. That is all any disciple needs to know.

Also, bear in mind that Jesus was not talking to "Christians" in this text, but to Jews. The question in their minds was whether they should listen to him or to his detractors who denied he was the messiah, claiming, instead, that he was a zealot who was threatening the foundations of Judaism. Jesus tells Thomas (and the others) that they can trust who he is just as he told the disciples of John the Baptist who went to Jesus on John's behalf and asked him if he really was the one they had been waiting for: "Jesus answered them, 'Go and tell John what you hear and see: the blind receive their sight, the lame walk, the lepers are cleansed, the deaf hear, the dead are raised, and the poor have good news brought to them. And blessed is anyone who takes no offense at me" (Matthew 11: 4-6).

Once again Jesus defines himself by values, not beliefs, just as he did in the Sermon on the Mount, essentially telling the disciples they can trust that values point to the will of God. If they live by them, they will show they belong to God and will be with God and he with them, just as Jesus was with God and God was with Jesus. In John's gospel, this is the point where Jesus begins to prepare the disciples for his death. He knows what is coming, but they don't, especially when the messiah was expected to lead a rebellion against Rome and re-establish the kingdom of Israel. That was not going to happen because that was not the kind of ministry Jesus was doing. He was a prophet of God, "messiah" in the sense of calling Israel to its vocation of showing the world the ways of God that consisted mainly of justice and peace. Jesus then tried to explain to the disciples that his ministry would not cease were he to die, but would continue through them ("Very truly, I tell you, the one who believes in me will also do the works that I do and, in fact, will do greater works than these, because I am going to the

Father" — John 14:12). This was the basis for hope, and his "preparation" involved getting them spiritually ready to be "with" him after he was gone.

None of what I have said touches on a more basic question about the authenticity of these words being from Jesus in the first place. As I have noted already, most scholars assign these words to the writer of John's Gospel instead of Jesus, for several reasons. For one thing, they underscore the role of beliefs Christians are to hold when Jesus didn't. Second, I have the same question about his being the only way to God that I have about his divinity. If Jesus wanted us to believe that, why didn't he say it multiple times and without equivocation? He wouldn't leave something this important to chance, would he? Moreover, why don't the other three gospels include the same words of Jesus found in John or at least similar ones? Finally, it is easy to slip into a literal reading of the Bible as an argument for the authenticity of Jesus saying no one "comes to the Father except by me," but that makes matters worse. Literalism means directly or indirectly God "dictated" the Bible.

Think about the impossible quagmire that puts you in. The Old Testament is written in Hebrew, and the New Testament is written in Greek. Words from one language often do not transliterate into another language perfectly. If God "dictated" or somehow intended the words of the gospel writers to be taken literally, in which language are we to understand them? The answer given is that language is no barrier to God speaking truth. At that point, the issue evolves into a matter of believing what the church or a group or a denomination or an individual says the Bible says, and we are back to square one, the problem a beliefs-based faith causes.

This discussion is important for several reasons, but the one most important here is that one of the fruits of a values-based faith is that it contributes to building bridges between people instead of barriers that inevitably arise because of differing beliefs. You and I may not believe the same thing about God, Jesus, religion, sin, salvation, eternity, and a host of other things, for example, but we can easily hold in common a commitment to being honest, treating people with respect, showing understanding and compassion for those in need, peace, justice, all the values that make the world a better place. This doesn't mean there are no conflicts over values. People have different values as well as different beliefs. Some people value self-sacrifice while others value personal success above all else. Some value simplicity while others value luxury. Some people value the spirit of the law while others value the letter of the law. The point is not that values cannot or do not cause conflict, only that values unite people while beliefs often become the basis for setting one against another.

An example of the difference a Christianity based on values and one based on beliefs is what has happened to the United Methodist Church. In February of 2019 delegates to the United Methodist Church's General Conference attended a called meeting to decide how it would view and treat LGBTQ members of the United Methodist Church. The Traditional Plan under consideration affirmed the Methodist Book of Discipline that condemns homosexuality as a sin and prohibits gay marriage and the ordination of LGBTQ candidates for ministry. An alternative approach also considered was called The One Church Plan. It would have removed the restrictive language of the Book of Discipline while adding assurances to pastors and Conferences whose theological beliefs prevented them from supporting same-sex weddings or ordain self-avowed practicing homosexuals.

The Traditional Plan was approved and the One Church Plan was rejected by the delegates. It was a vote that revealed the distinction between a values-based faith and a beliefs-based faith. The UMC Traditional Plan reflected the strongly held beliefs of its supporters. The One Church Plan reflected the strong commitment to values among its supporters. As such it was considered the plan that included a diversity of beliefs while maintaining unity among United Methodists. The Traditional Plan elevated faithfulness to beliefs above the pre-imminence of common values. Both sides were convinced their position was the right one, but their motivations could not have been more different. Traditionalists felt the urgency to take a stand on the beliefs United Methodists have held for many years. The One Church advocates were willing to set aside traditional beliefs for the sake of values that welcomed all, respected differences, and formed the basis for unity.

Perhaps the most telling irony of what has happened is that John Wesley himself knew that the relationship between values and beliefs carried the potential for the kind of division the United Methodist Church is now experiencing. In a sermon he once preached he was prescient when he declared: "Though we cannot think alike, may we not love alike? May we not be of one heart, though we are not of one opinion? Without all doubt, we may. Herein all the children of God may unite, notwithstanding these smaller differences. These remaining as they are, they may forward one another in love and in good works."[43]

Values are what make being of one heart possible. Beliefs don't. The Methodist conflict and division are typical of how the church has ignored this truth. For too long the church and most Christians have failed to understand the difference between a faith shaped by values and a faith shaped by beliefs, the result of which has been differences evolving into divisions one after another. At its core focusing on beliefs provides an excuse for not being sufficiently committed to living by the single most important ethic the Bible talks about—love. But not just any kind of love, unconditional love, which may be the most demanding challenge anyone can face in life. I explain why in the next chapter.

---

[43] (Sermon 39, 1872 edition, Thomas Jackson, Editor, https://www.umcmission.org/ Find-Resources/John-Wesley-Sermons/Sermon-39-Catholic-Spirit).

6

The Road Is Still Less Traveled

Focusing on living by the values Jesus lived and taught is a simple, yet profound change in understanding what it means to think of yourself as Christian. That's the good news. The challenge, though, is facing the fact that being Christian is more difficult than being **a** Christian is, not only because it is easier to believe something than it is to live by it daily. It also means you are living against the grain of the dominant culture whose values contradict most of what Jesus said. This is especially the case with the cornerstone value for Christian living, love. But not just any kind of love. It is love marked by unconditional grace.

In my experience such love is easy to believe in, but extremely difficult to practice. It is one thing to love another person. It is something beyond that to love them with an unconditional grace that goes the second mile when that is needed and gives them the coat off your back when they have none. In other words, unconditional love requires you to make sacrifices ordinary love doesn't. The gospels tell us Jesus spoke often about unconditional love:

> "I give you a new commandment, that you love one another. Just as I have loved you, you also should love one another. By this everyone will know that you are my disciples, if you have love for one another" (John 13:34-35).

> "For this is the message you have heard from the beginning, that we should love one another" (1 John 3:11).

"Beloved, let us love one another, because love is from God; everyone who loves is born of God and knows God. Whoever does not love does not know God, for God is love" (1 John 4:7-8).

These verses and others like them represent a call to a life of loving others, loving them unconditionally. This is the cornerstone of the lifestyle being Christian involves, something the Apostle Paul certainly understood: "And now faith, hope, and love abide, these three; and the greatest of these is love" (1 Corinthians 13:13). Paul was, of course, echoing the words of Jesus noted above (John 13:34-35) where he says love would be the way his followers would be identified. I think it is a reasonable conclusion to say that these texts are declaring that love is the primary value for defining what it means to be Christian.

Psychiatrist Scott Peck wrote about love being the heart of mental healthiness in his best-selling book, *The Road Less Traveled*, more than forty years ago. The book was and remains a seminal statement about the power of love to change your life and at the same time the forces within you and all around you that make living by love so difficult. He defines love as "the will to extend one's self for the purpose of nurturing one's own and another's spiritual growth," underscoring the thesis throughout his book that mental and spiritual healthiness are two sides of the same coin.[44]

Through his psychiatric practice he discovered that everyone is religious in the sense that everyone believes in something that gives their lives meaning and purpose. For many that is God, but it doesn't have to be overtly religious to illicit devotion.[45] Peck's definition lends support to the power of believing we have previously discussed. He also concluded that "grace" is at work in everyone's life, which he defines as "unconscious nudges" that help us achieve wholeness whether we sense them or not, nudges that are part of human nature, built into our DNA, so to speak. These nudges help us move "out of the microcosm into an ever greater macrocosm," by which he means learning to make choices that take us beyond what we know into something bigger, larger, beyond ourselves.[46] Essentially, Peck says, spiritual growth

---

[44] (NY: Touchstone Books), p. 81.

[45] Ibid., p. 185.

[46] p. 193.

is about gaining knowledge about ourselves, others, and the world. Faith comes after we have become learners.[47] Such growth is possible because grace is what makes "it possible for people to transcend the traumas of love-less parenting and become themselves loving individuals who have risen far above their parents on the scale of human evolution."[48]

While Peck believes grace is available to all people, his experience has taught him that not all people choose it for themselves, a phenomenon he cannot explain. In his words, "All of us are called by and to grace, but few of us choose to listen to the call."[49] Thus, spiritual growth always struggles against another side of our nature, the inclination to cling to what we already know. Peck says we must do the opposite, "distrusting what we already believe, actively seeking the threatening and unfamiliar...deliberately challenging the validity of what we have previously been taught and hold dear."[50]

He even calls this work the path to holiness wherein you question "everything" you know or believe because of a basic dedication to the truth.[51] Without such commitment, Peck believes, we cannot come to grips with the real world, choosing instead to live in our own fantasies, making it impossible to grow into spiritual maturity and emotional healthiness. He puts it this way: "The more clearly we see the reality of the world, the better equipped we are to deal with the world. The less clearly we see the reality of the world—the more our minds are befuddled by falsehood, misconceptions, and illusions—the less able we will be to determine correct courses of action and make wise decisions."[52]

This dedication to truth, he goes on to say, is the equivalent of having the discipline to work through life being difficult and full of trouble and suffering, and only mature love has that kind of commitment. Immature love, what I call "conditional" love, doesn't. That is why young love cannot last unless and until it comes to grips with the responsibilities enduring love

---

[47] Ibid.

[48] p. 300.

[49] Ibid.

[50] Ibid.

[51] p. 194.

[52] p. 44.

requires. Peck calls it "the myth of romantic love"[53] based on "the myth of falling in love."[54]

Getting Real about Love

You would think Christians would be the first to make the connection between reality and love, but, instead, we often weaken the demands of love by sentimentalizing it. "Why can't we all just get along?" is a common phrase that summarizes this temptation. The reason we all can't just get along is because immature love breaks down when confronted with the hardness of life, with reality. Newly married couples break up because they find out life is difficult, and they are not prepared to deal with it. The unreality of romantic love clashes with the realities of married life and they want to quit.

Yet, marriage is hardly the only symptom of people's lack of discipline in working on the demands of love. Interestingly, what makes the continuing popularity of Scott Peck's book counter-intuitive is that his experience as a psychiatrist convinced him that practicing unconditional love requires effort that most people are unwilling to give. That is why he calls a life of love "the road less traveled." At the same time, I can't help but wonder if the book's popularity suggests just the opposite, that more people than we might think are willing to work at loving this way because they want more than getting by or settling for the ordinary. Instead, they want life to be full and joyful, meaningful and purposeful and don't want circumstances to determine their future or difficulties to control their lives. At the very least it is the kind of life Christians who want to be more than a Christian, who want to be genuinely Christian, desire.

Loving the way Jesus loved, and the way he said we are to love others, speaks of unconditional love, love that is about the human will rather than feelings. In other words, it is about taking the road less traveled, a choice that is more difficult to make than it seems. That's because Jesus didn't call us to love our neighbor only. He said following him included loving

---

[53] pp. 91–93.
[54] pp. 84–90.

our enemies. I think if we are honest with ourselves, we will admit that these words of Jesus sound idealistic more than realistic. Indeed, instinct tells us to stay away from enemies, avoid them, at the very least not to trust them or be naive about the threat they pose, all of which at the very least does nothing to strengthen our resolve to treat them with more than contempt and suspicion.

But, of course, that is why this kind of love takes enormous effort. If it were easy, everybody would show it. It is no wonder that Peck says the critical factor in showing love is discipline, that is, the will to work with the tools available to us to grow in love, to grow toward mental and spiritual healthiness.[55] Because mental and spiritual growth is unavoidably painful as we confront ourselves honestly, everyone is tempted to give in to "entropy," or the human tendency to laziness, what Peck calls "the original sin." "So original sin does exist," he writes, "it is our laziness...No matter how energetic, ambitious or even wise we may be, if we truly look into ourselves we will find laziness lurking at some level."[56] Thus, he says all human beings heed the call of grace, that is, resist the nudges toward spiritual and mental health.[57]

If you choose to overcome the temptation to laziness, if you choose to take the road less traveled called love, the place to start is with yourself. Jesus said this when he connected loving our neighbor with loving ourselves. Healthy self-love is the key to neighborly love, but that is precisely why it is so hard to do. Self-love requires self-honesty, and self-honesty invariably leads to admitting our weaknesses, admitting that there are things about ourselves we don't like. Peck goes so far as to say that few of us avoid being neurotic or having some form of a character disorder.[58] Okay, but that doesn't mean we need to get into therapy before we try to live the way Jesus said we should or could live. It means, instead, that we do the work necessary to prevent our internal struggles, weaknesses, neuroses from controlling us to the point where we give up on the power of love, give up on the values Jesus taught and lived.

---

[55] pp. 15–16.
[56] p. 273.
[57] p. 300.
[58] p. 36.

Practically this is how working at loving others the way we love ourselves shows itself daily. It involves the discipline of self-examination wherein you reflect on the words you have spoken and the actions you have taken in complete honesty. After a disagreement with someone, for example, you would take the time to think about what role you played in it. How could you have changed the situation? How did you make matters worse rather than better? What can you learn from the incident that might help you avoid it happening again?

These are questions that arise from self-love. You care enough about yourself to want to be and do better. There is no higher form of self-love than the desire to grow beyond where you are, how you think, and what you naturally do that is less than desirable. What is more, that kind of self-love insulates you against vanity and self-centeredness. The best part, though, is that self-love of this nature allows you to be more balanced in how you see other people. An honest, balanced view of yourself is the basis for seeing others the same way. That is why you will, in fact, love your neighbor as you love yourself. Self-love is a necessary pre-requisite.

Finally, we have arrived back where we started, to the crucial difference between being **a** Christian and being Christian. Focusing on living a life of unconditional love is about values. Love as Peck defines it—"the will to extend one's self for the purpose of nurturing one's own and another's spiritual growth"—provides the substance for the kind of values you live by as someone committed to being Christian in the world. Extending yourself through compassion, justice-seeking, sacrificing for the good of others, honesty and integrity, these values make love real. You show you love your neighbor as you love yourself by showing compassion to her just as you would want her to show you in a time of need. You show love by telling the truth in circumstances that tempt you to be less than truthful. You show love by standing up for someone who cannot stand up for themselves. You show love is your aim when you choose to reject a tax break for yourself because you know it will end up being used to justify cutting food stamp funding for people who cannot afford to buy groceries without assistance. You show love by going the second mile, or even 240 miles.

That is what seventy-three-year-old Alvin Straight did. He rode a lawn-mower 240 miles to make things right with his brother. Alvin was a man living a very simple life in Iowa when he received word that his brother, Henry, had suffered a heart attack. Alvin was not in very good health himself, being diabetic, having emphysema from years of smoking, bad eyesight, trouble walking, and on top of all of that, he had to care for his mentally handicapped daughter, Rose. The news of Henry's heart attack was particularly troubling because the two of them had been estranged for more than ten years. His eyesight was too bad for him to drive himself from his home in Laurens, Iowa to where Henry lived in Blue River, Wisconsin, a journey of about 240 miles. He was too stubborn to ask someone else to take him, so Alvin did the unexpected, impractical, and what also seemed impossible. He decided to ride his old 1966 John Deer tractor/lawnmower to see Henry. He managed to hook up a trailer that hauled his gear and could also serve as a place to sleep at night, and then he set out on his journey.

The trip took six weeks and numerous turns and twists, all of which became the basis for a movie that told Alvin's story entitled, "The Straight Story," starring Richard Farnsworth and Sissy Spacek. Henry survived the heart attack, and after Alvin's visit, he moved to Iowa to be closer to family. Alvin's nephew drove him back to Laurens after he had made peace with his brother. And that is the heart of the story. The journey was the focus of the film, but the message was what happens when people sacrifice for the sake of love.

Colin Kaepernick showed that truth to the world when he lost his job as a starting quarterback in the National Football League after he decided to kneel on the sidelines during the playing of the National Anthem before the game started. It was a silent protest to highlight racial injustice in general and in particular the rising number of unarmed black men and black boys, some adolescents, being shot and killed by police officers. His actions became politicized when President Trump decided to make a public statement about the protest in which he accused Kaepernick of disrespecting the flag. In truth, Kaepernick was doing the opposite of what Trump said. His protest grew out of a profound love for his country, which led a man named Andrew Freborg who did not know Kaepernick personally to write a poem about it. As soon as the poem was posted on the internet it went viral:

> *I stand to honor the promise the flag represents.*
> *You kneel because that promise has been broken.*
>
> *I stand to affirm my belief that all are created equal,*
> *and to fight alongside you for that promise.*
> *You kneel because too few stand with you.*

I stand because we can be better.
You kneel to remind us to be better.

I stand to honor all that have fought and died so that we may be free.
You kneel because not all of us are.

I stand because I can.
You kneel for those who can't.

I stand to defend your right to kneel.
You kneel to defend my right to stand.

I stand because I love this country.
You kneel because you love it too.

As it turned out, Freborg's poem described Kaepernick's protest in the same way Kaepernick himself characterized it when he was named the recipient of Amnesty International's 2018 Ambassador's Conscience Award. Love is at the root of his resistance, he said, a collective love shared by others like his close friend Eric Reed who also took a knee that cost him a year of his career. Kaepernick pledged to those who gathered that he would not rest until his people were liberated from police violence and were treated with justice like all Americans should be. He then closed his remarks with these words: "Seeking the truth, finding the truth, telling the truth, and living the truth has been and always will be what guides my actions."[59]

In that brief statement Kaepernick brilliantly juxtaposed truth and love. Seeking the truth, finding the truth, telling the truth, and living the truth, that is the road less traveled. It is, in fact, the road everyone who desires to be in the world today the way Jesus was in his day will take. It is tempting to think the word "love" has become pedestrian, ordinary, unremarkable because it is so overused. But that can never really be the case. A life of unconditional love will always be extraordinary, remarkable, and never pedestrian.

---

[59] Kaepernick's entire speech can be viewed on You Tube at https://www.youtube.com/watch?v=5B8VU3JykvI.

7

The Real Rapture

The Latin root for the word "rapture" (rapere) means "to carry off" or "to catch up." Irish cleric John Darby created the concept of a Christian rapture wherein real Christians will take on their spiritual bodies and be taken up to heaven while everyone else is left behind to suffer the time of tribulation because they followed the anti-Christ. It is one of the silliest Christian beliefs ever imagined.

Given Darby's corruption of the word "rapture," I found it a bit odd that Joseph Campbell chose to use it in describing the meaning and purpose of life when he said it was the joy of experiencing "the rapture of being alive," by which he meant having "the experience of being alive, so that our life experiences on the purely physical plane will have resonances within our innermost being and reality."[60] Those are the moments when we feel the rapture of being alive, Campbell said, moments in which we experience the fullness of being human to such an extent that we have touched the very essence of life, the reason we are alive. At that moment we can be confident we have found our bliss, "that deep sense of being present, of doing what you absolutely must do to be yourself."[61] Bliss is when we are on the edge of the transcendent whose energy empowers us to be what we already are.[62]

---

[60] *The Power of Myth*, pp. 4–5.

[61] *Pathways To Bliss*, p. xxiii.

[62] Ibid.

This reminds me of something the great British preacher and psychologist Leslie Weatherhead once said about Jesus. He described Jesus as being divine because he was so fully human precisely because "divinity stands most clearly revealed and most perfectly understood in perfect humanity."[63] That, I think, is what Campbell meant by the notion that "the rapture of being alive" is the mystical moment when you have a sense of completeness, fullness, that happens when you live life at its deepest level and are, thus, connected to the transcendent.

It all sounds a bit heady, I realize, but the meaning of the phrase, "the rapture of being alive," is a truth that cannot be pursued. Its nature is to reveal itself because it resides deep in the human psyche already. You feel it, but you cannot explain it or find words sufficient to describe the richness of the experience. Yet it is as real as anything can be. The value of Campbell's perspective is that it points us to a higher level of thinking about what life can be, and especially a Christian life. We see glimpses of what he was saying in the world of art. It's like viewing a great painting, listening to a beautiful sonata, hearing a choir whose harmony and beauty takes your breath away, reading an inspiring piece of literature, or listening to a poem whose words stun you into silence.

Campbell himself had a spirit about him that suggested he knew first hand what it meant to experience the rapture of being alive. I read the book based on the Moyers-Campbell PBS interviews before I watched the series. but it was in hearing this great thinker talk to Moyers without a script that I was struck by the depth of Campbell's joy of life. What is more, he believed that it was human nature to desire to connect with the transcendent. This, to him, was the purpose of religion. He saw no value in pitting one religion against another, to say one is true and another is false. In his view religion was a sign of the best of human intentions to connect with the "beyond," something not to be explained or comprehended, only experienced. Campbell wanted his students to see that religion at its best was the desire to experience the rapture of being alive by discovering their personal bliss and following it wherever it leads.[64]

---

[63] *The Transforming Friendship* (Nashville: Abingdon, 1977), p. 65.

[64] *The Power of Myth*, p. 147; *Pathways To Bliss*, p. xxiv.

As a person of faith I affirm that this desire was instilled into us by God, but affirming it does not depend upon others sharing that conviction. In giving and receiving unconditional love, we touch the divine in all of us and in those moments become as fully human as we were intended to be. The traditional concept of original sin embedded in traditional Christianity gets in the way of this kind of vision, this call to living on a higher plain or at a deeper level. Just to be clear, the concept of original sin is the belief that the sin of Adam and Eve born of eating the forbidden fruit in the Garden of Eden permanently infected the whole of the human race. The blood of Jesus is believed to have been the necessary price God demanded to forgive humanity of its original sin.

This is the core of the salvation story Christianity proclaims as the "good news" of the death of Jesus on the Cross. Yet it stands in contradistinction to a prominent theme within Judaism, the faith tradition of Jesus himself, that speaks of the dual inclination for good (yetzer a tov) and for evil (yetzer a rah). The former makes life an endless struggle to overcome being human or the human condition. It is not about "being saved" from this evil body and all its debased desires and temptations. The latter takes human responsibility seriously in the choice to realize the full potential of being human or wasting it.

To love is to fully embrace the gift of life shared with one another, something Campbell said was another way of seeking to honor the God of our creation. Love is the key to experiencing the rapture of being alive. That experience does not exist outside giving and receiving love because love is the connection between God and God's creation. Believing in God is to believe we are the children of love.

The Jesus Connection Revisited

Years ago I wrote a book entitled, *The Jesus Connection: A Christian Spirituality*,[65] about the relationship Jesus told his disciples they (and we) could have with him. He used the vine/branch metaphor to help them understand what he was saying. They were to be connected to him as a

---

[65] (St. Louis: Chalice Press, 1997).

branch is connected to the vine as its life source (John 15:1-11). He also asked us to love him as God loved him, unconditionally. My conclusion was that following Jesus meant loving him, meaning, being devoted to him, and loving the way he loved as the way to show that devotion.

I have been asked if I still believe that. My answer is always "yes," but what I believe today leads me to be more precise than I was in that earlier book. Loving the way Jesus loved means living by the values he lived by. It is willful devotion to be in the world in a way that makes you determined to live by the values Jesus taught as a challenge to the dominant culture whose values could not be more different. As I have said, unconditional love is the premier value and represents the most formidable challenge to American materialism and all the injustices it creates.

Jesus concludes the vine/branch metaphor in John 15 with the words, "I have said these things to you so that my joy may be in you, and your joy may be complete" (John 15:11). The Greek word for "joy" has the same root as the word "grace." Some scholars interpret joy as the by-product of grace, the fruit of grace, if you will. The other word with the same root is "thanks" or "thanksgiving." In Greek it is "eucharistia," from which we get the word "Eucharist," the meal of thanksgiving. When the words joy, grace, and thanksgiving are put together, they describe the intended fruits of listening to and living by the words of Jesus, of being connected to him. Go the next step and you can see that the fruits of that relationship are no different from the values by which he invites you to live. Living by such values is precisely the way to enter into the "oneness" of all humanity, that mystical union born of the spiritual truth that at the deepest level of life there is no such thing as "the other."

Jesus said so himself in his parable about the judgment of the nations in Matthew 25:31-46. The standard by which we are judged in the eyes of God is simple—being a good neighbor, helping people when they are in need. Jesus went so far as to say that in welcoming the stranger, helping the sick, giving food to the hungry, clothing the poor, caring for the sick, visiting people in prison, were acts of compassion and love shown to him. He identified himself with people in need to the point where he and they were one person. "Just as you did these things to the least of these who are members of my family," Jesus said, "you did it to me." That was the standard. Jesus identified the reign of God with neighborliness. Be a good neighbor to someone is to be a good neighbor to God.

Debates about this parable often focus on the appropriateness of the social gospel being heart and soul of what it means to be Christian. I subscribe to that view, but that is less the point of the parable for me than the fact that Jesus was saying quite clearly that when we help someone in need we experience a "connectedness" to all humanity that includes his presence. Mystical as that may sound, it may be the fullest, most complete experience of the rapture of being alive available to us. Why? Because our lives are so intertwined with the lives of everyone else that when we meet them on life's most basic level of need, we experience the meaning of being one with the whole of humanity, and that connects us to the fullness of life. For people of faith we believe it connects us to God.

What I am saying is that being Christian is to touch the true meaning of what being human means because it arises from and is grounded in love. This makes sense and at the same time goes beyond the rational. That is because, as Campbell often said, religion is both rational and mystical, the way we as human beings enter into the mystery of life. It is the human way to conceptualize what words cannot express or capture. Religions are like poetry that captures human experience in words that point to it, but never fully encompass it.[66] That is why religions create myths and tell stories. They tell you who you are in the grandness of creation and, thus, how you are to live to show who you are.[67] Once the stories are concretized, though, measured and examined by facts and history, they lose their power to connect us to something bigger and beyond ourselves.[68]

Sacred texts may contain facts and history while neither ever being the point of any story. The point, rather, is to tell us about ourselves, about how to enter fully into being alive. Stories don't speak of absolute truth because, as Campbell said, "the ultimate cannot be put into words. It is beyond words, beyond images," conveying the penultimate truth, sufficient to put us in touch with our deepest selves, our spiritual core.[69]

Thus, the promise Jesus made is that we can know the truth, and in that knowing we will be set free to experience love, grace, and joy irrespective of what we may believe or don't believe about him.

---

[66] *The Power of Myth*, p. 174, p. 283.

[67] Ibid., pp. 262–263.

[68] pp. 25–26.

[69] p. 206.

8

Loving Sex

One of the ways to experience the rapture of being alive is in the act of making love, but you would never know it the way the church talks about sex. Almost everything the church has had to say about sex through the centuries reveals one very obvious truth—old white men, most of them unmarried—don't know anything about it, at least not anything healthy or wise. That in large measure is why sex is a subject few Christians are comfortable talking about, but all Christians think about. So does everyone else, of course, but the church's appalling ignorance about sex—and human nature, for that matter—is matched only by its determination to impose untold guilt on kids for having normal sexual urges. That is why when the church speaks about sex, no one should listen. That may be hyperbolic, but it doesn't miss the mark by much.

Not that I am an expert. I am not, but I do know a lot about what the church has said about sex and the damage it has done. First and foremost, the church made sex "dirty" by making it seem an evil urge to be resisted except when married. Silly beliefs such as masturbation being a mortal sin that could cause blindness was common when I was growing up. By the time I was a teenager I realized no kid I knew paid attention to what the church said about sex. It was the forbidden fruit everybody was tasting or wanted to, and no one had gone blind or been punished by God. I lived through the days when prudishness was the best adjective you could use to describe the church's attitude toward sex. Sadly, to this day it offers virtually no help to teens and young adults as they navigate the realities related to their sexuality. Worst of all, the church tells homosexual and transgender kids they are suffering from sinful desires they need to overcome, a message that has done immeasurable harm.

Given the church's attitude and teachings about sex for centuries, as one who is Christian you are better served by consulting experts in the field and learning from your own life experiences in order to form and reform your view about sexuality than listening to what the church says. I want to share some of my own for you to consider in this process, the first being that the same values that guide you in other actions apply to sexual relations. Loving your neighbor as you love yourself is chief among them. This means that your behavior in any sexual relationship should show your respect for the other person and your commitment to treating them as you want them to treat you.

This is an effective way to resist using your partner or spouse to satisfy your needs as if his or her needs don't matter. The question is, what do you need to do before making love that will ensure that making love is mutually consensual and co-equal. The wrong question is whether or not it was good for you or for your partner or spouse. That turns sex into a physical experience as if emotions involved don't matter. They *do* matter because emotional needs are always present and when ignored they hurt and even damage one or both lovers. For sex to rise above using another person for selfish gratification, you must be conscious of acting in a way that shows love for yourself and the other person.

Here, again, Peck's *The Road Less Traveled*, offers good counsel. He describes the love lovers share as one in which there is a temporary collapse of ego boundaries. Ego boundaries are the knowledge in our minds we develop in childhood through adolescence and even into adulthood regarding the limits we have physically, intellectually, and emotionally that define who we are and who we are not. We know our size, our physical limits, and our feelings. By the time we reach adulthood we live behind these ego boundaries in a state that feels lonely and isolating, made worse or better by experiences with others. He says the feeling of "falling in love" is, in reality, a moment when we experience our ego boundaries collapsing in connection with another person. It is the experience of being released from yourself into the other to the point where your identity and his or her identity merge. At that moment your loneliness disappears and you are overwhelmed with a feeling of being ecstatic.[70] Joseph Campbell might call this the apex moment when you experience the full ecstasy of being alive.

This is the kind of sex that happens only when your physical need and/ or desire for sex is not the driving force that brings two people together. Traditional Christian teaching attaches moral judgment on sex by insisting that such lovemaking is right only in the confines of marriage. Unless two people are married, the church says, transcending ego boundaries is not possible. We know that is not true. Marriage itself has nothing to do with it. The quality of the relationship between two people is the determinative factor. This is why "making love" happens in and outside of marriage.

Does this mean I am advocating Christians should have sex whenever they wish with whomever they choose? Of course not. In the first place, people, including Christians, are already having sex whenever they want to and with whomever they choose. Sexual moral prohibitions have never had any real impact on human behavior in any significant way. They have simply been the source of guilt and shame. I think using values as your guide instead of moral prohibitions is a more helpful and holistic way for you to think about sexual relations. Having sex is about how you are treating another person as much as it is about pleasure. Right and wrong should be judged on this basis rather than artificial limitations.

This is why traditional Christian teaching on homosexuality has been cruel rather than edifying. Same-sex couples are as capable of giving and receiving love as heterosexual couples are. The issue for them in having sex is the same as it is with heterosexuals. Is making love truly giving and receiving love, a moment when ego boundaries are transcended, enhancing the chance of lovers experiencing the apex of being fully alive? That standard has no sexual orientation attached to it. It is about this most basic human urge contributing to spiritual and mental healthiness. Christianity has not been kind to gays and lesbians and transgender individuals by impugning who they are and pushing them out of sight and into secret places to fulfill a human need for intimacy. Not all Christians have acted this way, but enough have to earn Christianity the reputation of being homophobic, not to mention hypocritical. Congregations and denominations that still judge people based on sexual orientation and gender carry the burden of teaching

---

[70] pp. 84–90, 94–97.

their members to believe falsehoods that have caused pain and suffering to others. If you are homosexual, you need never feel guilty about that. Traditional Christian teaching about you has been and remains wrong. I can say with every fiber of my being that being who you are is acceptable in the eyes of the God I believe in, and a God in whose eyes you are not acceptable is a false deity you have every right and reason to reject.

We know that sexual relations are a natural part of life. All creatures have the urge, but what makes sex among human beings more than animal instinct is consciousness of intimacy, a will to give love to another and receive it in return. Thus, the pleasure of genuinely "making love" transcends the physical pleasure involved because making love is what the experience is about. The irony of the church's position that sex is for procreation and, thus, limited to marriage, turns "making love" into raw sex. It is a perfect example of the way modern Christianity has allowed itself to be constrained by primitive thinking even as a more informed view of human life would be more helpful to its message.

The truth is, marriage has nothing to do with sexual relations. It is one context in which it happens, but not the only context, and as I have noted, sometimes not the best one. For the church to continue to insist that sex should be limited to marriage is akin to wishing upon a falling star. A 2007 Pew Research found that only 38% of all Americans believe premarital sex is in most instances wrong. Nearly 60% said it was wrong sometimes or never wrong.[71]

That percentage has remained stable in the last ten years. What is more, given human nature, some of those among the 38% who say sex before marriage is always or sometimes wrong have experienced it for themselves. The point is, the church lost this battle a long time ago, which means you have to find your own way on the subject. I have suggested letting love be your guide, but that is a decision you must make for yourself. What is important is making sure that your attitude and behavior regarding sex reflect your personal emotional and spiritual healthiness.

In 1979 psychiatrist Alex Comfort wrote a book entitled, *The Joy of Sex,* that became a blockbuster bestseller much the way *The Road Less Traveled* did ten years later. His book offered a direct challenge to the prudishness

---

[71] (https://www.pewresearch.org/fact-tank/2007/08/13/say-premarital-sex-is-wrong/)

of American Christianity that set millions of people, including Christians, free to enjoy the gift of sex as God had intended humanity to experience. The main reason for the book, Comfort said, was "to undo some of the mischief caused by the guilt, misinformation, and lack of information,"[72] much of which history makes clear came from the church. Instead of helping Christians, or anyone, discover the beauty of "unanxious, responsible, and happy sexuality,"[73] the church made sex dirty, taboo, talked about in whispers.

We are past those days in large part as a society, but the church lingers behind as if the wrath of God will come down on it for telling people sex was intended to be pleasurable. Part of the problem also lies in an unrealistic belief that telling people to ignore natural impulses and desires will get them to do so. It won't because it never has. People find their own way to satisfy their desires. That is why the wise path for churches is to help their members think in healthy and responsible ways. This is especially the case with teenagers. Not being open about sexuality has done nothing to help kids. Parents and churches have found this hard lesson to be true, the results of which have torn parents and kids apart.

This subject is important as you work at your own spiritual growth and nourishment because sexual relations is one of the areas where Christians encounter immense difficulty in feeling "right" about their sexual activity. I think one of the keys is to understand and accept the fact that most of what the church has said about sex for centuries has been wrong, wrong-headed, and sometimes mean and ugly. And the reason is precisely what this book is about. The church has approached sex based on beliefs instead of values. Its emphasis on rules rather than relationships lies at the root of its failure to teach Christians a healthy way to think about sex. Worse, it has led the church to do harm to its members, especially to its own children. I often wonder how many beautiful gay and lesbian teenagers would still be alive, perhaps with children of their own to love and nurture, had they not been told by the church that something was wrong with them. What if the church had been their refuge against the meanness they encountered in the world because of their sexual orientation instead of their accuser?

---

[72] NY: Crown Publishers, 2008, p. 6.

[73] p. 7.

I believe it could have been had the church focused on values instead of beliefs. Values offer guidance for sexual relationships instead of judgment, just as they do in all aspects of life, increasing the likelihood that sexual behavior will be responsible rather than promiscuous. That is the key to loving sex being about love more than sex, and making love a spiritual experience more than a physical one.

9

Putting Beliefs In Their Place

It has taken us a while to get here, but we have now arrived at the point of putting beliefs in their place, their proper place, to be specific. The underlying argument I have been making is that beliefs do not define the kind of Christianity that attends to the things Jesus said. This doesn't mean that beliefs don't matter. It means they don't matter as much as the church says they do, and not in the way the church says they do. They are important because they exert a significant influence on us. I can believe you are a person who is smarter than most people and that will make a difference in how I relate or respond to you. You can believe I am the dumbest person you have ever met and that will influence how you relate to me. Beliefs shape and reflect ideas and convictions that can help or hinder us. But they should not define what it means to be Christian. Values do that, not beliefs.

Allow me to put a finer point on this for the sake of clarity. There are two primary kinds of beliefs Christians hold without thinking about the fact that even though they are related, they are quite distinct from one another. One is theological. The other is moral/ethical. Church creeds are theological statements, assertions about God, Jesus, the Holy Spirit, the church, none of which can be proven, only believed. Moral and ethical beliefs, on the other hand, are convictions that may not be directly related to theological claims, but define what is right and what is wrong in human affairs.

Moral beliefs can be held in common without the need for people to affirm the same theological convictions. I may not believe all truth comes from God, for example, but believing in truthfulness can be a bridge between me and someone who does. A person who shows no regard for truthfulness is someone whose word few people would trust. That person might claim to believe in Jesus as the son of God and savior of the world, but those are theological beliefs that pale in importance when compared to his or her lack of moral integrity. A person of integrity, on the other hand, may not believe in God, but he or she does value truthfulness. That is why not all beliefs are the same kind. They can be theological or they can be moral/ethical. What they share in common is that neither can be imposed on people without conflict, division, and even schism. Both can help focus attention on values, but cannot serve as the glue that knits people together in community as values do.

Many Christians have discovered for themselves that people with different theological beliefs can be drawn together in community because they share the same moral values. I have friends who are Muslim and Jewish. We hold different theological beliefs, but we share common values. For that reason I feel a greater kinship with these friends than I do with evangelicals whose value system is very different from mine for the simple reason that they insist on making beliefs a higher priority than moral values.

My wife and I discovered the importance of building a community of faith based on shared values instead of common beliefs when we started a new church. One of our core values was freedom of thought, that is, the right to have beliefs others may not share. Our congregational covenant included a commitment to being willing to be stretched in uncomfortable ways precisely because we were a community where different beliefs were not simply tolerated, but encouraged. Moreover, this shared value, along with others, created a level of trust that allowed everyone to speak about their own beliefs without fear of censorship or silent disapproval. A values-based faith nurtures such an environment of trust which in turn allows freedom of thought to flourish. No one saw the desire for truth as a threat to faith. Just the opposite, in fact. Our community learned first hand that the pursuit of truth is not a threat, but is essential to spiritual maturity.

All of us must make the spiritual journey from childlike faith to mature faith. Being in a community where mature faith is valued and encouraged helps. In many instances this is found in a small group rather than the entire congregation, in part because the way some churches and church leaders react to questions about traditional teaching creates the impression that they would prefer keeping members in a perpetual state of spiritual childhood. Scott Peck says a healthy spirituality is possible only when you are willing to work at developing a religious perspective or realistic world view. That requires constant revision of your understanding of reality through new knowledge of ourselves, others, and the world around us.[74]

Beliefs and Human Nature

Beliefs can, of course, go beyond facts because that is how interpreting biblical texts works, but beliefs that contradict facts serve no useful purpose. Beliefs contribute to spiritual growth and healthiness when they call you to commitment rather than asking you to set aside facts and evidence that contradict them. Moreover, the common denominator when it comes to beliefs is that everybody has them, just as Scott Peck says everyone has a world view and, thus, has a religion. Not to believe something is to have a belief. There is no such thing as non-belief. That is simply not believing one thing while believing something else. Not to believe in God is at the same time believing in a random universe. Believing nothing lies beyond death is at the same time believing this life is it. Not believing the earth is round is at the same time believing it is flat. The list is endless, but the point is obvious. There is no such thing as non-belief, which is another reason why beliefs matter. That means you have specific beliefs, you believe in some things and not in others. The quality and worth of your beliefs depend on how they are affecting you.

That is what matters, how what you believe affects your life and the lives of others as I discussed in Chapters 1 and 2. Beliefs can be a powerful force in a person's life once they are embraced. They can determine life or death. That is what makes beliefs both important and at the same time dangerous. They have the power to influence people for good and for bad. That is precisely why they should never be set in stone, go unexamined, or be accepted uncritically. Beliefs lead us to do good things and they also lead us to do bad

---

[74]*The Road Less Traveled*, p. 191.

things. Beliefs can strengthen your commitment to the values Jesus taught or they can distract you from them, or, worse, undermine them. Several factors influence the role beliefs play in your life, none more than how you read and understand the Bible.

The Bible doesn't tell Me So

Because the Bible is Christianity's sacred text, how it is read plays a major role in whether or not you define your faith by beliefs or by values. The Bible is the source of authority within Protestantism, whereas authority within Catholicism is derived from church teaching. While the Catholic Church claims to base its teachings on the Bible, it is honest enough to say that what makes Catholics Catholic is their obedience to church teaching and practices. A parish priest focuses on Catholic creeds, doctrines, dogma, and practices when instructing the faithful. Put simply, the Catholic Church is focused on all things Catholic, not all things biblical.

In contrast, Protestant congregations and denominations teach and preach what they believe the Bible says. What many of them fail to understand is that at a basic level the Bible doesn't say anything until we say it does. This is why the statement, "The Bible says," can be very misleading, as was the case with America's beloved evangelist, Billy Graham, who used it regularly in sermons, books, and interviews. In doing so he unwittingly misled the American public, indeed, the world, about the nature and authority of the Bible. My intention is not to disparage Billy Graham's legacy. I heard him preach, read some of his books early in my ministry, and had enormous respect for him. That is why I am sure that were he still alive he would be the first to agree with me when I describe him as a man, a good man, a Christian man, rightly deserving to be admired by Christians and non-Christians alike, but a man nonetheless. That is why anything and everything he said was subject to the same mistakes and flaws as any of the rest of us, and on this score, his frequent use of the phrase, "The Bible says," could not have been more misleading and harmful.

The honest to God truth about the Bible is that it doesn't tell me or you anything until we begin to interpret it, a process that is unavoidable because that is how we process all external information. We interpret it.

Billy Graham could have avoided the confusion he caused had he simply added to the words, "as I understand it" to "the Bible says, something he, unfortunately, chose never to do.

Everybody who reads the Bible interprets it. It's a process scholars call "hermeneutics," which means "a method of interpretation." There are numerous hermeneutical methods, but in general they fall under two general headings. One is devotional reading, a legitimate and important exercise for Christians that is largely subjective, meaning you are content to believe what the Bible is saying to you personally. Whatever a verse or passage says to you is how you understand it. It doesn't necessarily speak the same message to someone else, but what matters is what it says to you and whether or not it helps you grow spiritually. My hundred-year-old mother read the Bible every day she could. She called it her "devotional time," a daily period in her day when she read the Bible for personal enrichment. That was enough for her. For some Christians, though, it isn't. They want to go further and insist that the Bible says what they understand it to say. That is where the trouble starts, in large part because what they say the Bible says may be very different from the conclusions scholars have reached through the use of the tools of higher-critical study, which is the second approach to reading the Bible.

Higher-critical study differs from devotional reading of the Bible because its goal is to get as close as possible to the original meaning and purpose of a passage of scripture. Special training that assists in the work involved in this interpretive process (hermeneutics) includes such things as efficiency in language skills, historical research related to the text and the intended audience to whom it was written, familiarity with various literary styles of writing used in scripture, and even insights from comparing similar stories found in different religions, and, of course, all the issues attending to problems related to translating texts from Hebrew and Greek into English (or German, French, etc.) without any available original manuscripts and only incomplete copies. All of these factors not only help the process of interpretation, but highlight why anything we say about a text is an interpretation.

In understanding the words of Jesus in the four gospels, three important questions add to the value of using both methods described above: (1) "What did Jesus' words mean to the people who heard them directly from him?" (2) "How did the people to whom the gospel was written years after

Jesus hear his words?" (3) "What do his words mean to us today?" These questions create a bridge between devotional and critical readings of the Bible. What a text may have meant to others in the past can inform our understanding, while at the same time how we hear the words of a text may provide us insight into how they were understood by people in different circumstances.

Canonical Criticism

Something else that helps hold the two methods together and adds to the value of the three questions above is "canonical criticism." This is a modern hermeneutical method that bridges the gap that usually exists between lay Christians and scholars. Canonical criticism works to understand the books in the Bible as they are, fully aware of the redactions or changes that the books have undergone without trying to get behind those redactions to some earlier version hidden beneath the given text. Canonical critics believe redactions are reflected in the existing text and that is the one most helpful in trying to understand what the Bible says. Whether Jesus actually said something, for example, is a question that is ultimately immaterial to what the text says he says. Arguing, for example, over whether or not Jesus spoke the words of John 3:16-17 or John 14:6 may interest some readers, but canonical criticism sees little value in that debate. It is, instead, focused on what the words the gospels say Jesus spoke meant to the people who first heard them, and also how we discern their meaning for our lives today.

Canonical criticism scholar James A Sanders says that the Bible itself asks and answers two basic questions: (1) Who are we? The answer is to be found in "muthos," or biblical stories (recalling Joseph Campbell's focus on the power of myth) that give people an identity. In short, they tell people to whom they belong. The second question (2) What are we to do? is about "ethos," lifestyle, ethics, about how we are to live.[75] These two questions are significant for several reasons. One is that they form a bridge between

---

[75] For an expanded explanation of these questions, and canonical criticism itself, see James A. Sanders, *Torah and Canon* (Wipf & Stock, 2005) and *From Sacred Story to Sacred Text* (Minneapolis: Fortress, 1987).

people of faith in the past and those of us today. "Muthos" and "ethos" refocus attention away from whether a biblical story is true or false to what it says about God's claim on our lives and how we are to live as people whom God has claimed. Canonical criticism sees story as an expression of people's need, desire, and hunger to connect with the transcendent, with God.

These two basic questions the Bible asks and answers are important reasons for resisting the oversimplifying of texts or using them as support for beliefs, or what is often called "proof-texting." They require thoughtfulness and commitment, knowledge and trust, a willingness to engage texts written by someone whose circumstances were different from our own. That brings us back to where we started, which is that whenever we declare that "the Bible says," we are ignoring all the reasons why reading the Bible for devotional enrichment is a valuable discipline, but hardly exhausts the full measure of what the Bible says, and can even become an impediment to it. But there is even more to this story that we need to discuss.

Pernicious Anti-Intellectualism

Complicating any reading and understanding what the Bible says is a persistent and pervasive anti-intellectualism that infects every field of study in modern life, but none more dangerous than religion. Perhaps the most comprehensive history of anti-intellectualism in America, including the role revivalist Christianity played in it, is historian Richard Hofstadter's Pulitzer Prize-winning book, *Anti-Intellectualism in American Life*. He provides an in-depth story of the meaning and origins of American anti-intellectualism that explains how we got to where we are today as a country and Christianity's role in that history. "Christianity has always seen a divide," Hofstadter writes, "between Christians who value the role intellect plays in religion, and those who follow the path paved by emotions."[76]

The former believe the latter group is always susceptible to preachers who play on people's emotions to manipulate them. especially when appealing for financial support. The American frontier, he says, was inevitably divided between "those who believed that intellect must have a vital place

---

[76] (NY: Vintage, 1966), p. 55.

in religion and those who believed that intellect should be subordinated to emotion, or in effect abandoned at the dictates of emotion."[77]

Because of its emphasis on a personal relationship with God, anti-intellectualism fit the spirit of rugged American individualism. Authentic encounters with God came to be judged solely by the authenticity of inward experience subject to verification only by the individual making the claim. Authority, Hofstadter points out, became fragmented, paving the way for charismatic preachers to be awarded authority by those listening to them because of the effectiveness of their appeal to people's emotions. He calls this phenomenon "the authority of enthusiasm"[78] that characterized frontier revivalism during the Great Awakening in the mid-1700s. A strong negative reaction among New England clergy to what they viewed as runaway emo-tionalism among Christians following the westward trails produced a split between intellectually based faith and anti-intellectual faith from which we have never recovered.

Signs of this schism are most clearly evident in the different ways peo-ple today read the Bible. Christians who reject the tools of modern critical study to understand the Bible by that very fact continue to make themselves vulnerable to being exploited by modern charlatans, such as "prosperity gospel" preachers. But the harm done by anti-intellectualism is not limited to high-level exploitation, as Hofstadter notes.[79]

Grieving parents whose nine-year-old daughter died from a staph infec-tion doctors did not catch in time do not find solace in hearing that God needed another angel and called their little girl home to heaven. The fact that such a comment was not intended to be hurtful does not make it less so. Good intentions do not negate the impact of bad theology grounded in anti-intellectualism.

That is the most damaging result of anti-intellectualism running through much of beliefs- based Christianity—the way the Bible is read and used—the result of which can cause you to abandon any value you see in the Bible. That would be a tragic consequence because the Bible is a marvelous

---

[77] Ibid.

[78] p. 57.

[79] Ibid.

witness to faith when it is read as such instead of as a historical record of God's relationship to the world, Israel, Jesus, and the New Testament church. If allowed to be what it is, a testament of faith, the Bible provides modern Christians with ancestral connections to their own struggles and triumphs. What stands in the way is a Bible made too small by people who have made what they believe about the Bible more important than what the Bible says. When this happens they become afraid of a literary device the biblical writers themselves used that can make the message of their words leap off the page when it is understood. That device is metaphor.

Metaphor is a figure of speech that means one thing is used to refer to something else, as if the two are similar. Unlike a simile that makes comparisons explicit with the use of "like" or "as," metaphors imply the comparison without making it explicit. This is one reason they are often taken literally. If I say my friend is as strong as an ox, I am saying his strength is similar to that of an ox. If I say, "You ox," and you take that literally, you would think I was saying you are an ox. The temptation to take metaphors literally happens frequently when it comes to the Bible. If we resist that temptation we can see that the Bible uses metaphors to paint pictures with words. Heaven is like a mansion in the sky with streets of gold and pearly gates. Taken literally that would be saying "heaven" is consumed by materialism. To say God is "Father" or "Mother" is to speak of God in terms we can understand, but to literalize that would be to force an image on God of our own making.

I think that biblical writers understood the meaning and value of metaphorical writing quite well. Some Christians today don't, so they literalize biblical metaphors and make them sound absurd. But the church has gone a step further and raised metaphors to the level of doctrine. Instead of speaking about Jesus as the "son" of God in a metaphorical way to attest to God being at work in his life, it has literalized that claim, turning Jesus into an actual offspring of God. To explain how that was possible, the church made Mary into a virgin who conceived a son by the Holy Spirit, literally, by God, making the "virgin birth" story a statement of fact Christians must believe in order to believe in the divinity of Jesus.

This is how metaphors that are incredibly rich and powerful figures of speech have been lost to Christianity. To literalize them has led to profound misunderstandings of wonderful biblical texts. That, I believe, has limited the power of scripture to offer spiritual nurture. In his editor's note at the beginning of Joseph Campbell's book, *Thou Art That*, Eugene Kennedy writes, "The spiritual needs of people are being neglected by religious leaders who insist on reasserting the historical-factual character of religious metaphors, thereby distorting and debasing the meaning."[80]

What Kennedy says points to an important reason why beliefs can get in the way of faith when they define its meaning and purpose. Hofstadter's history of anti-intellectualism in American life is indispensable in understanding the divide between evangelicals who are literalists and the rest of the Christian community. At the same time, it doesn't offer much encouragement that the divide can be overcome. Its history is too long and its schism cuts too deep. Just as I would never attend a church that had biblical literalism as an element of its statement of faith, I suspect biblical literalists would never attend a church that rejected a literalistic reading of the Bible.

More than that, there is solid evidence that biblical literalism makes the Bible less appealing to people rather than more, forcing them to believe things they cannot bring themselves to believe. The text that says God punished King Saul of Israel because he did not slaughter every man, woman, and child after defeating the Amalekite army (1 Samuel 15:1-35) is one example that comes to mind as a reminder that biblical literalism has served no noble purpose since it emerged in late 19th century. It is no wonder given the fact that it represented a misguided rejection of modern historical criticism in the name of protecting biblical authority. In this instance, the medicine was worse than the supposed disease.

The Bible has much to say to you and me and all Christians because its wisdom is virtually inexhaustible, but what it says depends on us, not on some artificial authority attributed to it. All that is needed for cultivating its richness is the will to explore all avenues of understanding to discern what the biblical writers themselves had to say. It is not a perfect science, but it does lead to great truths full of wisdom for people of every age. The Bible can remain a sacred text for Christians even as we seek to understand the meaning and significance of the testimonies of past generations using all the tools available for interpretation made necessary by the passage of time. As such, the Bible is a guide, not a rule book, a witness, not a constitution

---

[80] (New World Library, 2001), p. xv.

of beliefs binding on all Christians forever. As a sacred text, Christians can believe the Bible is a message written by people to people with the power to inspire and offer guidance and hope in new and ever-changing circumstances. It says nothing until you read it, interpret it, and listen to it. When you do that you sense the truth it speaks about how to be in the world in a particular way as one who has chosen to be Christian in all things.

Conclusion

My goal in writing this book has been to make the case that you can be Christian without believing everything the church or anyone else tells you. This doesn't mean that it doesn't matter what you believe, only that based on what Jesus said and did, Christianity is better defined by how you live than by what you believe. It seems like an obvious point, given the fact that human perceptions are what they are, human perceptions, with all the strengths and weaknesses they possess because we are human. For this reason, no creed, doctrine, dogma, or religious belief has ever or will ever transcend the reality of being human. If truth is infallible, we will never know it because human comprehension is always flawed. So the best we can do is to make approximations to the truth, aware as we should be that we can never grasp it fully.

As a person of faith, that is enough for me, even though the history of Christianity is one wherein at least since the fourth century Christian leaders have insisted on all Christians accepting the specific beliefs they said defined who was and was not a Christian. That way of thinking has persisted right up to today, sometimes unconsciously, but present nonetheless. In my own experience, and that of Christians I know, a beliefs-based Christianity has been a voice for conformity of beliefs rather than a source of the joy that Jesus said his words offered (John 15:11). Certainly, Christians have discovered the joy of faith anyway, but I would argue that in large measure it has been in spite of church teaching, not because of it. I am convinced that values are the key to joyous living.

Beyond its personal impact, though, a values-based Christianity also has the power to unite Christians because people have shown that they can agree on values even if they hold diverse beliefs. The efficacy of love, the pursuit of justice, showing dignity and respect for others, the power of forgiveness, the necessity of reconciliation as the foundation for peace; these and other values provide common ground on which Christians can stand. Beliefs do not possess this kind of power because the people who have them usually want everyone else to agree with them. That creates conflict and division.

I realize that focusing on values instead of beliefs will not satisfy all of us who claim the name "Christian," especially those who need a religion that provides a sense of certainty in a world where nothing seems stable anymore. But I must repeat what I have previously said, that certainty contradicts faith instead of supporting it. Worse, certainty closes the mind to the pursuit of truth, cutting a lifeline that faith needs to continue growing and maturing. As church attendance, or, the lack thereof, suggests, though, most Christians are not looking for certainty. They want the freedom to ask questions and to delve deeper into matters of faith. They view certainty with suspicion because that is what they have encountered in the church. I once had a banker who reminded me of this fact when he told me what he believed about a current issue that I knew was not the position of his Catholic Church. When I asked him how he dealt with the contrasting views, he said he went to mass and listened to what the priest said on some things and ignored the rest.

More typical than this banker are the thousands of Christians who have left the church, Catholic and Protestant. I will leave it to others to address that problem more extensively than I do here. My concern is more limited. It is to invite people in and out of the church who are still attracted to Christianity to trust a values-based Christianity to put you on the right path to living your life as authentically as Jesus lived his—a life grounded in love for God and unconditional love for yourself and others.

At the same time, a values-based faith extends beyond all of us individually to the role Christianity—and Christians—play in the world. A troubling by-product of Christianity being defined by beliefs has been a rigid exclusivism that pits one religion against another and has led too many Christians to insist that Christianity is the only "true" faith and all the others are inferior, if not false. This de facto declaration of the superiority of Christianity among the world's religions has been a persistent cause of social turmoil to the point of war. Unfortunately, as a beliefs-based Christian community, today's American evangelicalism preaches and teaches a similar kind of exclusivism that arises from a belief in the supremacy of Christianity.

A values-based Christianity avoids this kind of exclusivism, freeing Christianity to be a positive force in calling the world to peacemaking, joining hands with all people who share our values. When your faith is grounded in and expressive of universal values, what others believe is no threat to you. Working together for common goals across religious lines becomes natural, even inevitable. What is more, it shows the non-religious world that people of faith can get along, that we can transcend our differences, and that we can unite around shared values for the good of all. If I believe anything, I believe that is surely something Jesus would welcome.

A Word About the Appendices

These two appendices are included here with mixed feelings. What my personal beliefs are and what I think about the church have no direct bearing on anything I have written thus far, for two reasons.

First, this book is not an argument for any particular beliefs Christians should have, evangelical or progressive. In other words, I am not making an argument for a set of normative beliefs to replace those of traditional Christian teaching. Instead, I have sought to make the case for a Christianity defined by values that might actually allow Christians today to reclaim the diversity of beliefs that existed during the first three centuries of Christianity. Second, while it is difficult to talk about being Christian without talking about the church, they are distinct subjects nonetheless. Indeed, the church is a subject matter inextricably bound to a wide variety of issues that have no bearing on what this book is about.

All that said, because I stand within the Christian tradition intentionally, it seems appropriate that I should say something about what beliefs currently give me a place to stand in that tradition. Doing so highlights the freedom to explore a variety of beliefs everyone who defines Christianity by values will experience. The eclectic range of my personal beliefs about God, Jesus, the Bible, death and the afterlife, and so forth underscores both that freedom and diversity.

In regard to the church, it is a much more vexing subject for me to address. In truth, I have already written extensively about church and ministry in other books. What is most different here from those other writings is context. The torch of leadership today has been passed to a new generation of clergy, many of whom are my former students, though none of them should suffer from guilt by association. Where the church or churches go from here lies in their hands, something about which I share abiding confidence. I wish them well in the good work they are doing, and should anything I say here help them in it, that would be solely the by-product of grace.

Appendix One: My Story

Some of the readers of this material who are drawn to the concept of a values-based Christianity have asked me what I truly believe since I no longer believe much of what the church taught me. They have freed themselves from the anxiety they once had about not believing things they were taught or told to believe, but they are still searching to find their way when it comes to matters of belief. Several have said that my personal beliefs might provide some road signs as they try to find their way to their own place to stand. It is for this reason that I have chosen to include this chapter in the book. I have mentioned in previous chapters some of the things I don't believe anymore, such as Jesus being born of a virgin, Jesus being God, Jesus dying for the sins of the world, the whole idea of some people being saved while others are lost, whatever that means, Jesus coming back to judge the living and the dead, the Bible being the infallible word of God, to name a few. But none of that says much about what I do believe. This chapter fills that void.

The Matter of Jesus

I first put down in writing my beliefs about Jesus in my book, *A Different Jesus: A Christian Theology Big Enough for an Inter-faith World*.[81] That discussion,

---

[81] (Helena, MT: Sweetgrass Press, 2014).

however, revolved around the issue of the Christian doctrine of atonement, the claim that he died as a sacrifice for the sins of the world. Here I want to go beyond that issue and address more directly the age-old question of whether Jesus was different from us in degree or in kind. That is, was Jesus as human as we are, only more perfectly so in the way God intended for all humanity? Or was he both human and divine in a way that no one else is or ever has been, making him more like God instead of like us?

I first need to share a story that provides context for my answer to that question. It is about an experience in which I encountered what I think of as the mystery of faith. I have not encountered this mystery often, but enough to trust that it is as real as it is beyond rational explanation. The occasion was a weekend silent retreat I was leading for a group of my college students focused on the theme of peacemaking. On Saturday afternoon I was taking a solitary walk when the words came to me quite unexpectedly, "Jan, you cannot teach these students about peacemaking until you make peace with your brother."

I remember being confused by that thought, not least because I was not in any kind of open conflict with my brother at the time. The words would not go away so I decided to share them with the group as I led worship that evening. I told them that I believed the message I had "heard" was one to which I needed to pay attention, though I was not yet sure what that might mean. I had had enough experience with silence to trust that such unexpected thoughts were one of the ways God speaks to us today, that intentional silence was much more than the absence of noise, but was a way of listening to God. The challenge is to be sufficiently attentive to "hear" God "speaking." I believed then, and I believe now, that the experience I had on that retreat was one of those moments.

When I got home I called my brother and asked him to have lunch. His immediate response (which I later understood as quite telling) was to ask me what he had done now. I told him nothing, that I simply wanted to have lunch, but I knew it would be more than that. I had decided based on what I had experienced on the retreat that I needed him to know that as far as I was concerned we were brothers no matter what and always would be. Part of my motivation to say that to him was that as I reflected on our relationship after the retreat, I realized that I had not paid sufficient attention to the conversations he and I had had over the past year, when in joking ways he had let me know that he felt like I was always judging him. That was why he asked me what he had done when I called to ask him to lunch. You see, my brother was in a losing battle with alcohol that was having a major impact on our entire family, especially his children and my widowed mother. It had been going on for several years and I am sure I had let him know more than once what I thought of what he was doing. It didn't much matter how I said anything to him because I realized that in his mind the fact that I was a minister in and of itself added a dimension of "moral condemnation" to anything I said to him. I was "the good son" while he was "the black sheep" of the family was how he often put it.

The day we met we engaged in small talk for a while until I finally told him that I had asked him to lunch to let him know something I wasn't sure he knew or believed, that whatever was going on with him, he could count on me always being his brother. He asked me why I was telling him this now and I replied that I didn't have any reason except that I wanted him to know it. From that day forward I had regular contact with him as his life contin- ued to spiral downward. He most often called when he was drinking and would talk about how he knew he had messed up everything or was doing everything wrong. Predictably, he also managed to get in a word about my being the good son and his being the black sheep, and then when he would run out of steam he would hang up. Once in a while he called me during the day sober enough for us to talk about other things, mainly sports.

My brother never changed his behavior, and I stopped having any expectations that he would. We were brothers, and that was enough. When he died just before he reached his fiftieth birthday, I was at peace about our relationship. His life was tragic and ended that way, but I believe he died knowing that I meant what I said to him ten years before, that we were brothers forever. Many years have passed since then, and I still miss him.

Strange as it may sound, the experience I had on that weekend silent retreat—and similar ones—is why I follow Jesus. I felt something deep within me that I call the presence of God, a consciousness that I believe was—and is—the fruit of my devotion to thinking and pondering Jesus and his life. His words and deeds were then and are now the most tangible means by which I make connections with God. He is that conduit, that connectedness, that bridge between me and the transcendent dimension of life. Others may make that connection differently, but for me Jesus is the way, the truth, and the life.

At the same time, I don't think of Jesus as anything other than a man. His so-called "divinity" doesn't add anything to his life and teachings already being the tangible means of my connection with God. His relationship with God and my relationship with him are woven into the fabric of the mystery called religious faith. I was, of course, taught to believe Jesus was divine, different from me—from us—in kind, that he was God in the flesh. I spent years trying to understand Jesus from that perspective until I finally gave up. If he was divine and I am human, the challenge to be like him seemed to me to be a hopeless endeavor doomed to disappointment and subsequent guilt more than being filled with a sense of satisfaction and joy. If, on the other hand, Jesus was like us in every way and different only in degree, that is, he lived his life in a more perfect union with the will of God than the rest of us have achieved, but something of which we are capable, that would be a challenge worth taking seriously.

I opted for the latter, coming to believe Jesus was a prophet in the Israelite tradition of calling his people to covenant faithfulness and a rabbi in teaching a way of life that embodied that faithfulness in a singular devotion to doing the will of God. I also came to believe that Jesus believed such a way of life was possible for all Jews who understood their calling to be a witness in the world to the goodness, graciousness and redeeming work of God on earth. This is what I still believe about Jesus. His being divine holds no meaning for me because I have no actual understanding of what it would mean if he had been.

Divinity is a description of the transcendent, that is, what is essentially beyond the known and the knowable. What is known is that the way the man Jesus lived, and the things he taught, provide Christians with a tangible connection to his life. By living my life as he lived his, I identify with him. Had I lived in the first century I think I would have been a member of the Jesus movement, that group of Jews who followed Jesus without knowing exactly what to believe about him. According to Acts 1:6, where they ask Jesus if the time was right for him to restore the kingdom of Israel, it is obvious that their confusion about what to believe continued after the resurrection. That suggests to me that believing certain things about Jesus is not a pre-condition for self-identifying myself as Christian, and that is why I consider myself a "follower," not a "believer."

Salvation

Episcopal Bishop John Shelby Spong, not known for shying away from controversy, has said on more than one occasion that the church created "hell" to support its power and authority. In a nationally televised interview he explained why he believes this is the case:

"I don't think Hell exists. I happen to believe in life after death, but I don't think it's got a thing to do with reward and punishment. Religion is always in the control business, and that's something many people don't understand. It's in a guilt-producing control business. And if you have Heaven as a place where you're rewarded for your goodness, and Hell is a place where you're punished for your evil, then you sort of have control of the population. And so they create this fiery place which has quite literally scared the Hell out of a lot of people, throughout Christian history. And it's part of a control tactic."[82]

I agree with Spong's point, but I don't think he went far enough. "Hell" is part of the larger myth of "salvation" the church created that lies at the heart of its effort to wield authority and control over people in and outside the church. The promise of salvation to the faithful is the ultimate reward the church offers for its members listening to what the church says. That reward is called "heaven." By contrast, the loss of salvation is the ultimate punishment for those who don't. It goes by the name "hell."

In reality, the concept of "heaven" and "hell" lose meaning when the notion of traditional salvation itself is rejected. Salvation is a concept rooted in time and space neither of which has meaning in the realm of God. If God is, and if there is life with God after we die, that can only mean being in the presence of God without there being any way of not being in God's presence. That may sound complicated, but it isn't. What I am saying is that my choice to believe in God means I believe God exists without attaching to that belief notions of time and space that do not and cannot exist in eternity. By definition, eternity has no time or space, which is why it is a mistake

---

[82] Vic Bishop, "Retired Bishop Explains Why The Church Invented Hell," Waking Times, May 12, 2016.

when Christians literalize heaven and hell. If, on the other hand, heaven is the presence of God, that has meaning in this life of time and space as well as in eternity. The issue, then, becomes one of consciousness of God rather than divine judgment. Consciousness of God in this life logically suggests that consciousness continues after death. The reverse also makes sense. No consciousness of God now would make consciousness in any realm of existence after this life unlikely. In both instances God is present whatever our awareness may be.

The critical factor for my faith in thinking this way is that it maintains the image of God as love without weighing it down with the need for divine judgment, a concept born of historicizing religious myths and the power of gods to use humans as they see fit. Both Judaism and Christianity broke from this religious model by speaking about God in personal terms, as one who enters into covenant and responds to suffering and at the same time expects to be revered through faithfulness. This is the God I believe in, one I am willing to trust will hold me and the whole of creation in love, grace, and mercy. I don't need the fear of punishment to motivate me to faithfulness, and cannot figure why anyone else would either.

Life Beyond Death

My mother died at the age of one hundred. My wife and I cared for her in our home right up to the end. It was made easier by the fact that she was of sound mind and in reasonable health until her body wore out. That gave us the gift of quality time in which we talked openly about death, about heaven, about her being reunited with my father and my brother, with her mother and father, her brothers and sisters who had all preceded her in death, and even her first child, a boy, who had lived only four months. Did I believe all of this would happen? I can honestly say that I don't know. But I can also say that I wanted all of it to be true for my mother. Beyond that wish, who is to say what happens after death? It is speculation without any possibility of proof. Did I believe all she believed would happen? I did for her because that was the least I could do to support and comfort her as she faced the great transition.

The older I get the more I think about life after death. It may surprise you to learn if you do not already know that in my book, *A Different Jesus: A Christian Theology Big Enough For An Interfaith World*,[83] I make an argument for the bodily resurrection of Jesus. I won't repeat that here, but I can say that it begins and ends with my choice to believe in God. If God is not real, then, of course, that belief makes no sense, but for those of us who do it makes perfectly good sense. God being God means God has the last word in the continuing creation story which I interpret as the message of the raising of Jesus. It was a declaration that life here is part of the totality of human existence, but not all of it. The resurrection was God's message to the whole of humanity—not just Christians—that life in this realm of existence does not exhaust life as a whole. It continues.

You may disagree, believing that it makes no sense whatsoever. I understand the difference between us as proof that either of us could be wrong because claims of faith are beyond the reach of verification. That is why we can believe different things while remaining bonded by shared values. In the meantime I not only continue to believe in God, but that God is good, not unlike a parent who wants nothing but the best for her child. We are, as someone once said, the apple of God's eye, the love of God's life, the joy of God's heart. Thus, the good God I believe in would not limit life to this realm of existence.

An Unnecessary Exclusivism

Once I stopped believing Jesus was the only way to God, it did not take long for me to begin to wonder why I ever did in the first place. I don't understand why any Christian needs our way to be the only way. Ask Jews why they are Jewish when they have never claimed that Torah Law was the only way to God. It is the only way to being Jewish, but not the only way to God. Therein is a lesson for Christians. Jews have never understood themselves as the only people of God. Just the opposite, believing as they do that Yahweh is the Creator of the cosmos, making all people the people of God. As the

---

[83] (Helena Montana: Sweetgrass Press, 2015).

"elect" of God, their mission is to be faithful to the covenant God made with Moses and to witness to all people being called to honor and worship God only.

One of the unintended consequences of Christian exclusivism rooted in a beliefs-based faith is that it makes the influence of religion too limited. The Golden Rule, for example, is a major theme in all major religious traditions, a message that counteracts the forces of evil that seek to harm others in numerous ways. Given the power of evil in the world, to limit the Golden Rule to a Christian version is both arrogant and foolish, not to mention morally and theologically wrong. My view of faith is that it needs to be as big as it can be, as inclusive as it can be, and as humble as to make the first two things possible.

I also believe that values such as compassion, justice, mercy, kindness, forgiveness, reconciliation are an inexhaustible source of self-rejuvenation. My experience is that the more opportunities I take to put these values into action, the more healthy love I have for myself, which in turn helps me to love others unconditionally. That is the core of my faith as one who is Christian.

An Example of Good Religion

I believe there is such a thing as bad religion to an extent that I also believe some religion is worse than none at all. I believe at its core good religion points to the power of unconditional love to make your own life and the world better. The reason I am Christian is because I believe the values Jesus taught reflect that kind of trust. I believe good religion is informed by intellectual advance, scientific discovery, and discoveries about human nature and the human psyche. Good religion, put simply, is good for people, raising the sights of what they can achieve, be, and how they can help one another through life.

This is the kind of Christianity I wanted my children to learn about. I wanted them to see what being Christian looked like in real life. So when I drove a pick-up truck to deliver firewood to the poorest of the poor in our city as a participant in The Wood Ministry I helped to start, I often took my children with me. I wanted them to meet the men and women living in conditions my children did not live in. I wanted them to carry wood into homes heated by old tin heaters located in a small living room that was the only source of heat and in some instances for cooking. I wanted them to know that all the people they met helping in that ministry were doing so because they were Christians showing what being Christian meant.

That was one small part of the kind of Christianity I wanted my children to see. I wanted them to grow up believing that practicing compassion and justice was to follow Jesus. I wanted them to believe being Christian meant not judging others based on their economic circumstances, their immigration status, the color of their skin, or their sexual orientation. They heard preaching and teaching that taught this kind of faith, but I wanted them to see it in the lives of real people. I also wanted them to learn that being Christian should influence how we manage our family's resources, including helping others financially even though we did not have money to spare. Because I was an educator, I wanted them to value a good education and to believe that being Christian and good thinking were compatible, a faith defined by values with beliefs consistent with those values. It is a faith that can out-think the world, something one of my teachers used to say was as important as out-living the world. I want the kind of faith I live to be teachable to others, especially children. When my children were small I believed that the greatest contribution I could make to the world would be to raise up young adult Christians who wanted to give to the world more than they take from it. That challenge was all about right values, not right beliefs.

People Matter Most

Core to what I believe about the message of Jesus, the life of Jesus, everything we know about Jesus, is that people matter most. How could his words be understood to say anything else? Indeed, because God is Creator, putting beliefs before people could be described as the equivalent of playing God. No belief is impervious to human flaws and that should be enough to convince anyone that putting beliefs before people is a fatal mistake God would never want anyone to make. Beliefs stand on shifting sand as new insights are gained and new discoveries are made. That is why beliefs change. As an adult, you don't believe today what you believed when you were a child.

Once again it is worth recalling the words of the Apostle Paul when he said: "When I was a child, I spoke like a child, I thought like a child, I reasoned like a child; when I became an adult, I put an end to childish ways" (1 Corinthians 13:11). I have found that being a mature Christian requires a lot of things being put away because of what the church has taught and still teaches.

The sum of all these parts, then, is that I seek to be Christian in my words and deeds based on the words and deeds spoken and done by Jesus of Nazareth, a man of God, dedicated to God, living for God, and inviting me to follow him by doing the same. Because of who he was, I believe God is loving, compassionate, forgiving, and seeks to use us to help one another. That is how I understand God's participation in the world. God has put good in us, and each time we follow its impulse we make the world more God-like. We make the world better.

The Trouble with Sin

In 1973, psychiatrist Karl Menninger wrote a book entitled: *Whatever Became of Sin?*[84] Recently I came across an article by a psychologist named Abe Abercrombie who believes Menninger was prophetic in seeing the future we are now witnessing. The future that Abercrombie believes Menninger saw was one in which the word "sin" would no longer be used, replaced by rationalizations excusing individual accountability. Menninger suggested words such as illness, disorder, dysfunction, syndrome would replace "sin" based on the belief that being human was the product of biochemistry, environment, experience, and trauma. If this happened, Menninger thought, no one would be responsible for their choices and conduct. That day, Abercrombie says, has arrived.[85]

Really? With American prisons overflowing with the largest population in the Western world, heavily tilted with minority populations, Abercrombie thinks people are no longer being prosecuted for crimes. Statistically,

---

[84] (NY: Hawthorn Books, September, 1973).

[85] Abe Abercrombie, "Whatever Became of Sin?" an article posted on the BCI website, April 25, 2013.

that is true for white Americans, especially when it comes to "white collar" crimes. Paul Manafort, former chairman of the Donald Trump's 2016 presidential campaign, was sentenced to four and a half years (47 months, of which he will serve 36) for eight felony counts involving bank fraud and money and income tax evasion that involved tens of millions of dollars. The day before Manafort's sentencing a client of public defender Schott Hechinger was offered a sentence of 36–72 months for stealing $100 worth of quarters from a residential laundry room. Another woman was given a six-year jail sentence for voter fraud because she was a convicted felon who didn't know she couldn't vote in her state. Yes, white people, specifically, white men, get away with committing crimes, but I don't think that's what Abercrombie had in mind.

What he did have in mind was using Menninger's book to augment his Christian claims as an evangelical whose primary credentials are that he believes the Bible was inerrant and infallible in its original text (of which we have none) and that Jesus Christ died for the sins of the world. It is quite predictable that "sin" would be a serious concern for Abercrombie who is a counselor for the evangelical Biblical Counseling Institute. Menninger, on the other hand, focused on the danger of providing a psychological justification for not holding people accountable for their actions. The agendas are quite different.

I share Menninger's concern, but the word "sin" is too toxic to be helpful today in talking about personal accountability. That probably sounds strange coming from a minister, but in talking about my faith I have to confess that the label "sin" does not hold meaning for me in the way it once did. The word in Greek means "missing the mark," an apt and accurate description of the way I live along with everyone else. We miss the mark all the time in relationships, in words we speak, in judgments we offer, in decisions we make, in any and all things. "Sin," in the sense of a description of the human condition, is a useful term, but its theological connotations have all but rendered it unusable to me. The Bible speaks of it frequently, as does the church, as have Christian theologians in every generation. But have we reached the point where the term serves no good purpose?

I think the answer is "yes." Traditional Christianity teaches and preaches a message burdened by questions it cannot answer because its basic claim tests the limits of reason. I think the word "sin" is another name for doing wrong, not being wrong. It is another name for "doing harm," for being selfish and self-centered, for saying things that should not be said, all of which are wrong because they hurt others and ourselves. When we do harm to another, we harm ourselves because we are making the heart of God "ache." "Sin" is anything that makes God's heartache, which makes our heartache, too, because God is a part of all of us.

This way of talking about "sin" makes sense to me, but the notion of God making Jesus pay a price for our sins in order to forgive us projects an image of God which if I had to believe would lead me to give up faith. From my perspective, "sin" is a problem in terms of what it reveals about one side of human nature that wants to harm and hurt, but that is less of a problem than the one the church has created by using "sin" as a justification for its abuse of people via its awful judgmentalism and exclusion. A more pointed way to say it is that the problem of "sin" is that the church has used it to cover up its own "sins" so that the best thing to do about it is to call it what it is, "missing the mark."

Going Deeper Still

In Chapter 2 I told the story Corrie ten Boom told about being in a German concentration camp after she and her family were caught hiding Jews in Holland. She described the power of believing in Jesus as "there is no pit so deep that he is not deeper still." Going deep is a helpful description of what growing spiritually means. Because I believe in God, I then believe going deeper into ourselves is an apt description of experiencing God. God is in us as God is in all of creation. The deeper I can go into myself, the richer the experience of God. Further, it is this inward work that holds the key to remaining committed to living by the values Jesus lived and taught. The call to living Christianity, to being in the world in a particular way, can wear you down. At least that has been my experience. I have felt like giving it up more than once. Resisting climbing the ladder of ministerial success was always a major challenge for me. So was turning the other cheek, working for justice, loving a neighbor who turned out not to be all that loveable in the first place.

What is more, I was incredibly naive about the bad inclinations that lurk inside of ourselves. In spite of church teaching about Jesus dying for our sins that assured us of a place in heaven, being a Christian has never made and never will make Christians more virtuous than anyone else. Perhaps one reason so many believe it does is because of the notion that becoming a Christian changes your life dramatically. A few call it being "born again," but most think of it as making a significant change in your life. It can happen and does happen, but in my experience, it doesn't last long. The yetzer a tov (inclination for good) and the yetzer a rah (inclination for evil) to which I referred earlier in the book continue to battle to gain control of the human will. The evidence is rather obvious. Christians act as evil as non-Christians and non-Christians act as pure as the best Christian. This is why church history is so checkered. The church has always been led by Christians who have done good and evil in every generation.

Closer to reality is the fact that human beings do possess the inclination for good and the inclination for evil. Each of us chooses which one domi-nates our thinking and our behavior. It is a choice that must be made over and again. The one way we can tip the scales toward good is to nurture that side of our nature, to engage in spiritual practices that strengthen the urge to be right and do right, overpowering the urge to be vindictive, unforgiving, unloving, selfish. It is called "the inward journey" that consists of spiritual tools or disciplines such as silence, meditative prayer, devotional reading of scripture, fasting, spiritual direction, and others. These practices deepen our daily consciousness of God which in turn helps us to ask what we believe God would have us do in all situations in life. Spiritual practices don't make us perfect, but they do make us better. They help us do right by being right with God, with ourselves, and with others.

When I began to discipline my spiritual life through practices other people recommended, I was surprised by how difficult staying on the inward journey was. As it turns out, "doing" is easier than "being." Yet, our doing soon runs out of gas when the energy and vision for it is not replenished by nurturing our spiritual life, our being. Even more, the inward journey gives credibility to the outward journey and also keeps it honest.

Spiritual practices form the foundation for inward spiritual strength in numerous ways, none more critical than self-reflection. I have found that self-reflection not only helps me resist the temptation to nurture my anger over injustice, or the desire to give up and quit the struggle, it also brings me up short when I fall into self-pity and self-righteousness. Worse than people being wrong on an issue of human rights are people who are right and self-righteous about it. The Apostle Paul confronted this problem among the Christians in Corinth who were dividing into groups gathered around the teachings of different early church leaders such as Paul, Apollos, Peter, and others. His warning is blunt: "None of you will be puffed up in favor of one against another" (1 Corinthians 4:6). The inward journey has proven to be an effective way to avoid getting "puffed up" as I seek to do justice work.

It is also the key to surviving the worst of times spiritually. Because life is hard, as Scott Peck said, maintaining spiritual balance is anything but easy. Personal difficulties throw us off balance. My experience is that staying faithful to doing the work of inward spiritual grounding is how I keep my spiritual bearings. The same holds true when life outside my personal world goes to pieces, much like it is in America today under Trump's presidency. I have lived through many tragic and traumatic times our nation has gone through—the assassinations of President Kennedy, Martin Luther King, Jr., Robert Kennedy, Vietnam, the fight against segregation and for civil rights for all—just to name some of the most obvious ones. The inward journey is one way I have found that strengthens my attachment to God and empowers me to detach from the results I am seeking outwardly. I never stop caring about those results, but when I am spiritually grounded I am better able to let go of the disappointment when they fail to materialize.

Attending to spiritual practices, then, has become essential to my outward involvements. In the end I think that is how I have been able to strive toward being Christian in my words and deeds rather than being content to call myself **a** Christian. To be honest, at this point in history I think the elementary standard by which all Christian beliefs should be judged is that they do no harm. That would go a long way in tempering the damage Christian beliefs have done to the people who hold them and to others around them. This is why beliefs are important. This book is my effort to limit the harm they do.

Appendix Two: The Church Has a Story Too

Throughout this book I have used the phrase "the church" with some justification, as I will explain below. Yet, in reality there is no such thing as "the church," most especially when it comes to Protestantism. At best we are talking about groups or, better yet, groupings of churches, when we say "the church," which means that in practical terms "the church" does not actually exist. When I use the term "the church," you could rightly ask, "Which one?" They number into the thousands. That is what makes it so difficult to say anything meaningful or worthwhile about "the church." Criticism or praise of it might be widely off the mark when it comes to your particular congregation, or it could be spot on.

On the other hand, the challenge of talking about the church might not be the crapshoot it seems to be. There is a sizeable record of "the church," with a large body of writings and historical events sufficient to allow us to speak of "the church" with a certain credibility. Moreover, even though the Protestant movement that emerged in the 1500s quickly became very diverse, the many different groups nonetheless did hold enough in common, then and now, to allow us to speak of "the Protestant Church" with a measure of credibility. My reluctant attempt here to write about "the church" is more narrowly about that, the Protestant Church, though there is no "wall of separation" between Protestants and Catholics that would prevent anything said about the one having implications and applications for the other.

I say that as a Protestant, and of a kind that was born on the American frontier and adopted for its own theology and practices the concept of the autonomy of the individual that is endemic to American democracy. In other words, I have a denominational heritage that is thoroughly American, a factor that may have in no small part played a role in the churches of my tradition—along with many others—being in decline. At the same time, there is a better than average chance that my concern about the inaccuracy of the term "the church" doesn't matter that much to you anyway, not least because you may not attend any church or care about what is happening to it. If that is the case, you are one among many, and the reason this book is about Christianity rather than the church per se. I have already alluded to the fact that the majority of Christians have left the church and the vast majority of Americans pay no attention to it.

There are sociological categories for church dropouts. The SBNL are the "spiritual but not religious," mostly Millennials (between 23 and 38), the NONES are the "not affiliated or nothing in particular," and a new group that is called the "DONES." These are people who were once very active in a church, but have now dropped out altogether with no plans of going back. In short, they are "done" with church. What is more, "the Dones" are not young or young adults. They are primarily in their senior years, some early seniors and others advanced, and more than a few are retired clergy. We once called all these groups by one name, "church dropouts." While sociological analysis has made advances in identifying who they are and why they are who they are, the impact on the church is the same. People are gone, absent, not seen very often, or not at all.

The rise of these groups underscores the dis-ease that exists in most congregations, but that dis-ease is hardly monolithic. Many people are not sure why they no longer feel connected to their church, but they don't. It just doesn't interest them anymore. Some of the ones I know feel a theological void that has existed too long without getting any substantive help from the church to fill it. They were told to ignore their questions and "just believe." Others are tired of doing the same thing the same way it has always been done and seeing the same results they have always seen. Still others find attending largely boring and perfunctory.

If you attend church at all, and it happens to be Methodist, Presbyterian, Episcopal, or the like (i.e., "mainline churches"), more likely than not you are in a congregation whose best days are behind it. In other words, your church is not the congregation it used to be. If, on the other hand, you attend a non-mainline church (none of the above), then you are probably in a congregation that is growing rapidly and may have already reached the status of being called a "mega-church." This means you are in a congregation that is filled with young people and young adults with lots of children whose best days seem to be ahead of it.

There are, of course, exceptions to every rule, but I think it is safe and accurate to say that in general this is the current state of American churches. Those in decline are generally mainline congregations (or what theologian John Cobb calls "Old Line")[86] and those growing rapidly are generally not mainline (though some may have been at one time). For convenience sake, we might call them New Liners or New Mainliners. Even at that, practically speaking the phrase "the church" is more anachronistic than accurate in referring to Christianity in America today. What is more, the diversity of "churches" further complicates the task I have set for myself, but it is one I have nonetheless chosen to undertake.

A major influence on how I think about the church is the fact that I have been in it all my life. I cannot remember a time when I wasn't. It is not an exaggeration to say that the church has been my whole life. It has been the source of some of my greatest joys and some of my worst disappointments. Because of the church, I have known some of the finest people in the world, people whose lives are genuinely inspirational. I have also known people in the church—clergy and laity—who have made me want to run as far away from it as I could get and be done with the whole enterprise.

I think a critical factor in assessing what has happened to churches in America is the fact that being pushed to the sidelines has been no accident. The high dropout rate is an inevitable consequence of the way they have acted throughout history, and certainly here in America. In numerous ways churches have earned the position they now occupy of being largely ignored not only by the dominant culture but by Christians themselves. These days Christians still in the church wonder what the future holds. My sense is that nobody knows because no one can know the future.

---

[86] John Cobb, *Reclaiming The Church: Where The Main Church Went Wrong and What To Do About It* (Louisville: Westminster John Knox Press, 1997), p. 6.

More than that, my view is that asking whether or not the church will survive is the wrong question. There is reason to believe it will in some form, but the core question is whether the church's survival actually matters. Is its survival critical to Christianity? To American society? To the world? If it is, I think it will be only if the church confronts the ways being an institution hinders and distorts its life and mission. Most church leaders and informed church members I have known admit that the church could do better than it does, but little seems to change.

If anything is to change, I think it will necessarily be on the congregational level because this is the point of genuine intersection between Christianity and people's lives. If history is prelude, we have seen already that denominations are too large and theologically divided for significant change to happen. More hope for change resides where people are in congregations that often have weak ties and even less interest in their denominational ties. This is not to say change at the local level is likely because it isn't, but if it does happen, I think that is where it will happen.

The Church and Me

In the interest of full disclosure, I should describe my current relationship to the church as a way to put what I am saying in context. My wife and I both wear the label in our denomination of being retired ministers in good standing, a status that is reviewed and renewed yearly. Beyond that, I suppose it would be accurate to say that neither of us has much of a substantive relationship with the church. We have a vital and dynamic relationship with Christianity, just not the church. We are members of a congregation, but our involvement is limited to supporting it financially. That is because after retiring, our spiritual hunger and needs led us to gather a group that would meet in our home for worship. We knew a few people who had been active in a church at one time, but were no longer. We let them know what we were planning to do and invited them to join us on the first Sunday of this new adventure.

That was four years ago and we continue to meet weekly. Our group remains small with an average of about 18 people who attend regularly. We discussed the decision to do this with the regional leader of our denomination where we reside who affirmed what we were planning to do. We did not require his permission, but we did want his support and were grateful he gave it. The members of our group fit the label "Dones" referenced previously in the sense that all of them once attended church, most all their lives, but are now "done" with it. Our worship is more casual than what you find in churches on Sunday, and includes time focused on discussions around scripture texts in place of a traditional sermon, but essentially it is the kind of worship in which any Christian would feel at home.

We have no expenses, but we do collect donations that are spent on meeting social ministry needs we learn about, such as paying rent for people, buying books and clothing for children, providing Christmas for four to six families yearly, and supporting causes beyond the local area related to poverty and environmental issues. We have said from the beginning that we do not want to become a church and have stayed firm in that commitment. We keep no records and people are free to come and go as they choose. Over the four years we have been meeting we have had a few people to join us for a while and then drop out, but the core of the group has remained stable. It meets our spiritual needs and that seems to be enough at the moment, but we stay open to whatever change may come our way. We are taking it one week at a time.

This new ministry is consistent with a lifelong struggle and at times conflict with the institutional church. It began with an incident early in ministry when the congregation I was serving lacked the spiritual maturity (I say that with no disrespect) to respond to a member in serious need. At the time everything seemed to be going well, except that I realized the problem was not the people themselves so much as the way they had learned to be a community of faith from years in the church. I knew at that moment that if I had been there nine years rather than nine months doing what I was doing, the same thing would have happened. Suddenly I went from thinking about climbing the ranks of the clergy ladder of success before me to wondering why I was a minister at all.

Fortuitously or providentially, it was precisely at this time that I was introduced to the Church of the Savior in Washington, D.C. that was established by Gordon and Mary Cosby. Their vision of what it meant to be church challenged everything I knew about church. That's a story of its own, but the important point here is that the Church of the Savior changed my life and the direction of my ministry forever. Organized in opposite ways from the traditional business organizational pattern of committees, boards, trustees, and officers most churches have, Church of the Savior opened my eyes to a whole new way of thinking about congregational ministry. I came to believe as I still do that traditional congregational structures fit a church content with maintaining institutionalized religion, but drain the life out of one that desires to live its life by the values Jesus lived his. The truth about church life today is that the typical congregation has turned in on itself as it has become consumed with maintenance ministry that has pushed mission aside. Making matters worse, most congregations make their decisions by voting. If there is anything more inimical to being church than voting, I don't know what it could be, producing as it does "winners" and "losers" rather than community.

I believe that at the heart of what is wrong with churches today is deadly institutionalism that forces congregations into measuring success the old-fashioned way, by size, money, and power. Church of the Savior taught me what I should have learned growing up in the church, that none of these matters in the eyes of God, that a church can be large, wealthy, influential and still betray the gospel. I know because my home church did exactly that in the face of the call to racial justice, just as churches today are committing a similar betrayal in the way they think about and treat people based on sexual orientation or gender. I often describe my experience at and with Church of the Savior as the moment when I got saved from the church.

That sounds hyperbolic, but it is as close to the truth as I know it. Those were formative years for me as a young minister during which I learned that having a renewed spirit is not enough to effect permanent change in church life. The reason is simple. Structure is as important as spirit, a fact in my experience few ministers or lay people have ever believed. I suppose I continue to hope against hope that they will, but if that is to happen I believe it will take more than most congregations seem willing to give, and to give up.

The task, then, is to talk about congregations where the survival of the church making any real difference is most likely to take place. But let's be clear. There are no steps to this end worth writing about. If anything, describing steps that can change the church tends to trivialize the enormity of the challenge. But how do we talk about it? My approach is to suggest some broad challenges that if taken seriously by congregations have the potential for assuring that their survival will genuinely matter to their members, communities, and even denominations. There are no "steps" that will make what I am suggesting more possible. What follows are a few ideas congregational leaders might consider as they seek to find hope for the future.

• • •

The first one is to rethink the mission of the church from spreading the gospel to teaching the gospel. A renown preacher of a past generation once wrote that the largest field of evangelism was sitting in church pews every Sunday. He was talking about the fact that the attitudes and actions among church members made it quite clear that when people join the church they are not necessarily committing themselves to being Christian. I saw that first hand in my home church that not only accepted racial segregation as a way of life, but practiced it as a church. The "separate but equal" principle of law in my native Virginia was another name for racism, but my hometown pastor and his wife whom I loved dearly believed it was a morally justifiable policy and so did most of the people in our very large congregation.

Becoming a member of my home church and becoming a Christian had little to do with one another when it came to justice or loving your neighbor as you love yourself. We were a living example of the bifurcation of being a church and being church. We believed our responsibility was to make disciples of everyone (Matthew 28:19), which meant getting them to come to church.

What we didn't understand was that we first needed to learn what the gospel was before trying to tell anyone else about it. That need remains paramount in churches today. The focus remains on ways to grow churches as if that means something. My home church was the largest in our city and among the largest in our denomination. Looking back on our practice of southern segregation, it is clear that growing our church had little to do with living by the values Jesus taught.

Dietrich Bonhoeffer wrote in *The Cost of Discipleship* that when Jesus bids a person come follow him, he is bidding that person "to come and die."[87] That is hardly the message congregations preach because they know it is unlikely to get many people to join the church. Instead, they believe you have to get people in before you can get people "in." In other words, employ the best marketing techniques to attract people to come to church and then try to persuade them to become Christian. It may sound reasonable, but it doesn't work. Willow Creek near Chicago, the flagship of mega-churches, decided to find out if that strategy produced the results they believed it did. They hired an independent research firm to do a study and the results were clear. Getting people into the church as the first step to getting them to become Christians in attitudes and lifestyle was a failed strategy.[88]

Experts in the field of group dynamics have known this for a long time. People who come into a group for one reason seldom continue when the purpose of the group changes. More than that, the strategy of getting people "in" as a way to get them "in" flies in the face of Jesus telling all would-be disciples that the first step in following him was to deny themselves, followed by picking up a cross (Mark 8:34). It is still the same message because living by the values he taught creates conflict with the dominant culture, along with family and close friends. That is not a message easily incorporated into modern evangelistic methods pastors and congregations have been taught. That is why I have been convinced for many years that the church growth movement of several years ago that still exerts influence did enormous harm to the integrity of church membership and the credibility of the Christian message.

One of the most urgent needs in congregations today is to stop trying to spread the gospel and focus time, energy, and resources to learning what the gospel is and then making the conscious decision to embrace its values or close their doors. Without that kind of commitment, the existence of Christian congregations is pointless. It, in fact, guarantees that the survival

---

[87] (NY: Macmillan Paperbacks, 1963), p. 99.

[88] "Willow Creek Study Says Church Programs Don't Work," (https://chuckwarnock-blog.wordpress.com/2007/10/24/willow-creek-study-says-church-programs-dont-make-better-disciples/)

of the church will not matter. The irony of how congregations usually think is that people respond proportionally to the challenge put before them. Ask little of people and that is what they will give. Ask a lot and they will give that. Development staff in colleges and other organizations learned through experience that donors don't usually give what they can, but what they are asked to give. Ask for hundred dollars when the donor could have given a thousand and you will get a hundred.

Commitment of any kind works this way. The gospel is demanding, claiming your whole life, but the only way you can discover its worth is to give your all. This is what congregations need to teach, but leadership has to first learn it and then be willing to risk teaching it. It is time for churches to let numerical growth take care of itself. I learned from the Church of the Savior that the strength of a congregation lies not in numbers, but in commitment. Congregations willing to trust that will refocus their mission to teaching the gospel instead of spreading it. They will, in turn, discover that the most effective way to spread the gospel is to live it.

* * *

A second step for congregations that want their survival to matter is to teach a Christian message that focuses on the values Jesus taught instead of beliefs about him. To avoid repeating what I have already said about beliefs and values throughout this book. I want simply to underscore that the difference between these approaches to faith is not benign. I think it has been one of the primary reasons so many Christians have dropped out of church. They didn't like being told what to believe or an environment that did not welcome questions. Churches that are afraid of critical thinking about matters of faith and morals are too afraid for their survival to matter.

Putting values before beliefs creates a greater chance for Christians to enjoy the vigor of theological discussion and debate because the only thing at stake is learning. Once no one's fate in the eyes of God hangs in the balance based on beliefs or the lack thereof, there is an incredible freedom to learn theology. That is one of the first things seminary students discover. It may be unsettling for a short time, but they always discover the value of being in a learning environment where no idea is out of bounds, no text is so sacred as to be off-limits for scrutiny, and where they learn that the most important qualifications for ministry are a sound mind, a benevolent heart, and a soul filled with empathy for all. This is the kind of environment that should permeate every congregation. Church members would thrive in it. Quitting would be the furthest thing from their minds. It is a paradox that the church thought it could hold on to people by seeking conformity of beliefs when all that was needed was the practice of love that included trusting people to think for themselves.

Theology, that is, the study of God, is the church's vocation. This suggests thinking is not an enemy of faith, nor even tangential. It is essential, in fact, endemic to genuine faith, making an environment of open inquiry and honest pursuit of every idea indispensable in a congregation's life. I don't think anyone would argue that this is the kind of environment usually not found in churches. More likely to be found is a resistance to open inquiry and fear of theological debate. Yet both are critical to the development of spiritual maturity.

Certainly in the early centuries of church history there was a time when the church needed to establish boundaries around Christian beliefs, but once that had been accomplished primarily with creeds, church leaders should have been wise enough to see that the future depended on how well Christians lived instead of how right their beliefs were in the eyes of church hierarchy. By then, though, power and authority pushed out trust in love. Coercion and conformity became the preferred tools of persuasion and love became a word used to paint over a multitude of sins. That kind of church authority is anachronistic in the modern world, most especially in a nation like ours where freedom is a value above most others. In short, believing what the church says because the church says it no longer carries authority and influence, forcing congregations to rely on example rather than words for its message to matter.

• • •

A third step is for congregations to stop throwing people away. The world already hurts people and causes them pain and suffering. The church shouldn't be adding to that number. The world already marginalizes people. The church shouldn't be doing the same thing. No one should be judged for being different. Doing that is a fool's game and a clear indication of the extent to which congregations have been shaped by the world. I think of all the kids who have grown up in a church knowing that everyone around them would reject them immediately if they knew they were gay or lesbian or unclear about their gender or were different in some other way about which they could do nothing.

Recently I read a statement by a Christian who said the church has managed to teach him just enough to make him not want to go to church. The story below is an example of why many church members and clergy feel the same way:

> I was recently fired from my job as a chaplain at a Christian university for officiating at a same-gender wedding of a former student and colleague. I was fired because some within my church and my school were shocked that I could be so "scandalous." Others quickly proclaimed the need to punish my act as treasonous and expel me, "the immoral brethren," from the church. Still others have practiced the subtler religious art of shunning. Even as a 48-year-old, heterosexual, married, white, privileged and resourced evangelical, I've found that "coming out" in full support of the LGBTQ+ community has been a brutal experience.[89]

When I first read these words I got angry. How could I not? When someone describes the experience of supporting a marginalized group such as the LGBTQ+ community as a "brutal experience" because of the reaction of other Christians, you have to take notice. Joy and I had heard more than a few stories like this when we established the new church. Part of becoming a member was participating in what we called a spiritual life group for new members. It was our chance as pastors to share the vision for the kind of community of faith we were trying to create, what it was, how it functioned, and why it was different from churches they may have experienced before ours. It gave new members a chance to share their spiritual autobiography, their story about their spiritual journey that had brought them to our community. On several occasions, we were brought to tears as gay and

---

[89] The Rev. Judy Peterson, "Why I sacrificed my chaplain's job and my reputation to marry a same-sex couple," Religion News Service, March 6, 2019: (https://religionnews.com/2019/03/06/).

lesbian new members described the rejection they had experienced from one church after another and sometimes from their family members. One lesbian couple candidly told the group that because of past experiences they were afraid to leave their infant daughter in the nursery during worship the first few times they had attended our church. When we asked them why they said that based on previous experience they were afraid we wouldn't give her back. That broke our hearts.

No one should ever feel that way when they go to church, but this is what congregations have done to people because of their sexual orientation or gender. It contradicts every value Jesus taught. Churches have got to stop hurting people, stop making them feel as if they could be thrown away. No belief can ever justify such un-Christian behavior. Any congregation that does this sort of thing is one whose survival can never matter. That is why it is essential that congregations realize that bad behavior by a congregation is more than an individual transgression. It is a systemic problem whose roots lie in a fundamental misunderstanding of what Christianity is. The only power that can override a belief that harms and hurts people is for values such as love, justice, mercy, kindness, and compassion to be the highest priority of communities of faith.

● ● ●

Congregations that want their survival to matter also need to let go of the need to achieve success as defined by American culture. In spiritual terms, success means servant-hood, sacrificing on behalf of another, giving instead of trying to receive, none of which is possible without a renewed dedication to faithfulness whether it leads to "success" or not. Let me tell you the story of a congregation that made that choice.

The Church of the Covenant in my hometown of Lynchburg, Virginia began a very successful day camp on its grounds in the 1950s that drew upwards to a hundred kids for each of the six summer sessions. The church was located in a well to do neighborhood from which Camp Kum Ba Yah drew most of its campers. On July 4th, 1961, six black boys and an adult civil rights leader tried to buy tickets to one of two "whites only" pubic swimming pools. The pool manager immediately closed the pool, and the next day the city announced that all three city pools (two all-white, one all black) would be permanently closed. Within days each one was filled with dirt and covered with concrete.

Hearing what had happened, Church of the Covenant pastor and Day Camp Director, Beverly Cosby, said publicly that the camp pool that had always been open to the public would welcome everyone. A few days later some black children accompanied by an adult came to swim. They did without incident, but the next day the camp attendance for white kids dropped to zero. The financial base for the camp was immediately in jeopardy, but the Church of the Covenant remained firm in its determination to practice racial justice. Those were difficult days for the camp, but fifty years later the Camp is going strong, fully integrated, allowing it to bring together kids from privileged neighborhoods and kids from the inner city. What is more, Church of the Covenant stood as a beacon of light to other churches that had yet to garner the courage of faith to reject segregation and openly welcome people without regard to race.

This is what faithfulness looks like. Yesterday the issue was race. Today it is sexual orientation and gender. Tomorrow it may be immigrants and undocumented workers. The issues may change, but the church is called to be faithful to the values Jesus taught in all circumstances. Congregations that are committed to such faithfulness can have confidence that their survival will make a difference to the church as a whole and in the world.

* * *

I also believe congregations whose survival will matter will need to redistribute their resources. Most congregational budgets are heavily tilted toward expenditures on salaries and maintenance. The size of buildings and staff has grown while the outreach of the church has stagnated or declined. For centuries Christians have built buildings too large and too ornate for the glory of God, as if that made sense. Today they are called "campuses." One church in my area spent fifty million dollars on its new "campus" of buildings, all to the glory of God. But God's world is filled with people who are poor, hungry, naked, without medical resources, without basic human needs. Worse, anti-poverty organizations say that we have the technology and the resources to eliminate extreme poverty in the world, but lack the political will to do so.

The signs suggest that this is also the case with church wealth and financial resources. I believe the church needs to begin divesting itself of buildings and reinvesting those resources in working with groups around the world committed to eradicating extreme poverty. We may have the poor with us always, but we don't have to have extreme poverty. Governments can help eliminate it, but the church could take the lead. It in fact should. But that is not likely to happen, unless it is willing to take steps to diminish the power of institutionalism and embrace the truth that "success" in churches begins and ends with an engagement with the poor right where they are and in ways that often call on churches to sacrifice for the sake of that engagement. The nature of the sacrifice is not always monetary. It can also mean risking being criticized or losing members, but whatever the sacrifice it serves as a reminder that being Christian carries a cost.

There are creative ways to change church culture away from building buildings to focusing on mission, but sometimes, if not often, leaders lack the will. Having been in church leadership for decades I am confident in saying that as long as churches de facto teach their members to "go to church" rather than "being the church," nothing of substance is likely to change. To be a member of the Church of the Savior you must belong to a mission group and practice spiritual disciplines like prayer, silence, Bible reading daily. If you do not want to do these things, you cannot be a member. They are quick to say their way is not the only way to be church, it's just their way. The church has never been large, and today is made up of small sister communities with missions groups. Anyone familiar with the Church knows its reputation as a community involved in numerous missions such as a medical clinic for low-income families, a home for terminally ill patients, low-income housing support, political action on capitol hill, especially on behalf of economic and racial justice, and many others. The sister communities spend over a million dollars a year in their work, yet most of them have unpaid pastors and leaders of mission groups. I would say that the best way to describe the Church of the Savior is that it knows the difference between being a church and being church.

That holds the key for the church's future to matter. Unless and until congregations consciously choose between being a church (an institution or organization) and being church, survival is a benign question. What has already happened to congregations should have told leaders that years ago.

Today there are millions of post-church Christians in America and around the world, most of whom were part of the church before dropping out. Whether that is a good or bad thing for Christianity remains to be seen, but it is not a good thing for the church. Worse, the church has no one to blame but itself for the predicament it is in. As it turns out, what the Apostle Paul's said about individuals reaping what they sow is also true for institutionalized Christianity.

One of my favorite preachers of a past generation who was also a bishop in his denomination used to tell the story that a layperson came to see him to talk about the state of their denomination. The lay elder was unrestrained in the criticism he made. When the man finished the bishop thanked him for coming to see him, and once the visitor had left he said to himself, "Thank God he doesn't know any more than he does." I used to laugh when he told that story and whenever I repeated it. Not anymore. Too many years have passed with too little change in the church to laugh today. What the bishop said was a de facto admission of the failure of the church to do better than it was doing.

This doesn't mean I think the church is all bad, or bad at all. As I have said, I have known some of the finest people in the world in the church, people I have wanted to be like. But I suspect they were who they were and are who they are in spite of the church, not because of it. I am sure that is an overstatement, but not by much. The church does much good and the church does much harm. It has helped and hurt people, given them a reason to live and made them feel like something was wrong with them. At the end of the day, though, most congregations, and certainly all denominations, have spent too much money on themselves and too little on being in the world in a particular way shaped by the values Jesus taught. This is where institutionalism has caught up with the church in ways that have virtually undermined its reason to exist. If there is a future for congregations that matters, it will have to be one in which resources are directed away from the church and into the world.

* * *

Finally, and perhaps more important than anything else I have said, the future of congregations and the church as a whole will matter only if they take the need for moral credibility more seriously than they do now. Churches have lost credibility in the eyes of the American public and now we have the documentation to prove it. Even more, we now have evidence that partisan evangelicalism is a major reason why. A recent Gallop survey shows that during the past 20 years church membership has gone over the cliff with a 20-percentage-point decline since 1999.[90]

More than half of that change has happened since 2010. Journalist David Crary interviewed Notre Dame Political Science Professor David Campbell who studies religion's role in U.S. civic life about the survey results. Based on his research, Professor Campbell concluded that politics plays a major role in church membership decline, describing it as "the allergic reaction many Americans have to the mixture of religion and conservative politics." He went on to say, "Increasingly, Americans associate religion with the Republican Party—and if they are not Republicans themselves, they turn away from religion."[91]

Crary also spoke with Mark Chaves, a professor of sociology, religion and divinity at Duke University, who noted that as recently as the 1970s it was difficult to predict someone's political party by the regularity with which they went to church. "Now it's one of the best predictors," he said. "The correlation between religiosity and being Republican has increased over the years."[92] Chaves's observation explains why among the 25% of Christians who still attend church, the majority are white evangelicals, Of that percentage, only 8% of Americans ages 18–29 self identify as "evangelical,"[93] while members of progressive churches make up the bulk of the 75% who have dropped out. Not even church members listen to what the church has to say anymore because of the loss of credibility.

Of course, other factors are contributing to this decline in church membership, but all of them arise from or point to the issue of credibility rather than relevance. People don't trust the message churches preach because they are appalled by what churches say and do. A heavy portion of the

---

[90] Jeffrey M Jones, "U.S. Church Membership Down Sharply in Past Two Decades," April 18, 2019 (https://news.gallup.com/poll/248837/church-membership-down-sharply-past-two-decades.aspx).

[91] David Crary, "Poll: Church membership in US plummets over past 20 years," Associated Press, Minneapolis Star Tribune, April 20, 2019.

[92] Ibid.

[93] Michael Gerson, "Why White Evangelicals Should Panic," Washington Post, August 29, 2019.

responsibility for people being repelled by churches rather than attracted to them lies with evangelicals. Professor Campbell says young adults especially are suffering from "an allergic reaction to the religious right." He further explains, "One of the main rationales for the very existence of this movement was to assert the role of religion in the public square in America. And, instead, what's happening in that very movement has actually driven an increasing share of Americans out of religion."[94]

A by-product of evangelicals baptizing conservative policies as if God is on the side of Republicans is that mainline or progressive ministers are facing the challenge to persuade their congregations to live the gospel, especially regarding our nation's social, economic, and political life. When a large number of Christians adopt the Machiavellian ethic of the ends justifying means in public, as evangelical support for Donald Trump illustrates, people of values stop listening to them. What the Gallop survey cited above reveals is that the damage this kind of political partisanship has done goes beyond an impact on evangelicalism. Mainline congregations have also been swept up in the disgust people have for organized religion. When the Christian message sounds more politically partisan than Christian, the damage done is enormous, if not irreparable.

One of the reasons mainline churches have suffered collateral damage is that they have made the same mistake evangelicals have by defining Christianity by beliefs instead of values. Many progressive churches talk about the social gospel, but few draw the distinction we have in this book between being a Christian and being Christian. This has left them to criticize partisan evangelicalism politically, but not theologically. The problem with the former is certainly its partisanship, but that mistake is rooted in a theological exclusivism that makes being a Christian defined by beliefs more important than being Christian defined by values. Only the future will tell what will happen to congregations and the church as a whole, but this much we can know. Going forward no congregation can assume that its credibility is a given. It must now be earned. The only place to begin that work is to start talking about values and stop trying to force conformity of beliefs on anyone who wants to be in the church.

* * *

---

[94] Ibid.

We have now arrived at the point where we started, my offering thoughts on the church of no real consequence, and perhaps no value. From a distance I watch what is happening in and to congregations, to the church as a whole, with the feeling that for me the end of this movie is a repeat of the beginning. When I began ministry I was fortunate enough to learn from a creative and dynamic community of faith that institutionalism was a deadly enemy of being church. What I know today to a far greater extent than I knew then is that a beliefs-based Christianity is a critical reason ecclesial institutionalism is so resistant to change or reform. As a result, Christianity has become a cacophony of beliefs and creeds and doctrines and dogmas that makes what Jesus said and did unrecognizable.

Yet, even in the face of deadly institutionalism, I worry about the future of the church because the world could benefit from its witness to both transcendence and the oneness of all humanity. I have given my life to the church in the hope that I might make a difference in the way it lives and moves and has its being. I am content to leave the judgment as to my success or failure in that regard to others, focusing instead on worshiping and serving with the others in our small Sunday morning worship group for whom this book was both written and dedicated.

CPSIA information can be obtained
at www.ICGtesting.com
Printed in the USA
BVHW042135160220
572515BV00003B/10

9 781627 342926